Characters
on the
Green

Everyday Golfers are the *Real* Character of the Game

Charlie —
Hit 'em straight!

J. Peter Hoyer

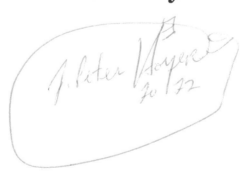

J. Peter Hoyer
70/72

outskirtspress

DENVER, COLORADO

Outskirts Press, Inc.
http://www.outskirtspress.com

ISBN: 978-1-4787-5631-6

Outskirts Press and the "OP" logo are trademarks belonging to Outskirts Press, Inc.

PRINTED IN THE UNITED STATES OF AMERICA

Table of Contents

Prologue

Legendary basketball coach John Wooden once told his players, "Your reputation is what you're perceived to be by others, your *character* is what you really are. You're the only one that knows your character. You can fool others, but you can't fool yourself." To his comments I would add that actions reveal your true character.

Amateurs who play the game of golf are some of the most fascinating "characters" on Earth. Why else would someone wear polyester plaid Bermuda shorts with a striped polo shirt and white calf-high socks for no other reason than to play this game? And in public, no less.

Golf has unique qualities that draw folks from all over the world to the game. Take a moment to consider these quirks about the game. Why is a player limited to fourteen clubs? Why does the little ball have over three hundred fifty dimples on it, and how do they help? Why, when you swing to the left, does the ball fly right, and why, when you swing to the right, does the ball fly left? Why are there eighteen holes to play, and why is every hole only 4.5 inches wide? Why is the green called "the green" when the entire course is green? Why is golf even considered a sport when you can ride all over the place and never sweat a smidgen as you would playing other sports? *And* you can drink beer and smoke cigars or cigarettes while playing. In all other sports the higher score wins, but in golf you lose. Why?

Don't look for those answers here.

Maybe, just perhaps, there aren't any explanations. Or, as my high school history teacher would tell us, "You can look it up."

One thing is for certain, though. You will meet interesting people on the golf course. Most are friendly, some are not. Others are weird, some are strange. As proclaimed by Jonathan Eig, author of two sports-oriented books, "In storytelling, it's character, not the bounce, flight, or spin of the ball, that drives the plot." I couldn't agree more.

When Dr. Seuss wrote, "Oh, the places you'll go, the people you'll meet," he may have been thinking about the times he played golf.

My old golfing buddy, Patrick, and I often meet strangers on the golf course. Paired by the starter, we play along together for several hours. These guys are your average everyday players, and camaraderie is important for us in order to have a pleasant day. Most players are interesting, some are boring, but everyone has a story to tell. As Patrick and I recall the day's round at the nineteenth hole, we find ourselves laughing about the "characters" who play this game. "The stuff we hear from these funny guys would make an interesting collection of stories," he once said. After some deep thought about this idea while repeatedly tapping my forefinger on my chin, I hatched my idea to write about these peculiar anecdotes.

With Patrick's hint of inspiration, along with my forty-year history of stalking fairways, accompanied with strange stories from unusual pairings on golf courses, I share with you these true stories of everyday golfers. Even though Patrick offered his usual deadpanned one-liner to discourage this writing—"It ain't gonna happen—" he said, it actually had the opposite effect on me.

It is also with thanks to my granddaughter, Zoey, age nine, who taught me how to properly send a text message, and my daughter, Sarah, with her one-line text, "URsofunny," that I got started on this book.

You see, not long ago I purchased a cell phone with the capability to send unlimited text messages. My previous phone was almost exclusively used for making and receiving phone calls. Merely eight to ten years behind everyone else in America, I am finally catching up to the civilized world. My newer phone is nothing like a "smartphone—" it's more like a "dumbphone." Before sending my first-ever text message, I asked my granddaughter, Zoey, to give me a lesson on the contraption. Girls, I found out, love to play teacher. After a thirty-minute lecture, I was ready to join the free world of talking and texting. Then she gave me my first test—to type and to send a text message. My first message was short, a simple "hello" sent to my daughter, Sarah, to inform her that I was now capable of messaging, and not just one or two messages, but unlimited messages, all month long. I received her reply and immediately answered back. "I can txt now babyyyyy." Her answer was a straightforward, "URsofunny." My golf-weary wife, upon seeing my reaction, laughed her head off. Her head didn't actually pop off her neck, but if it had, we'd be in the *Guinness Book of World Records*. "First woman ever whose head popped off while laughing."

Carol, my non-golfing wife, also repeats this mantra, but usually when she says, "You're so funny," it's accompanied by a smirk, a warning, and a shake of her head. Some years ago when I suggested to her that the manufacturers of shampoo and hair conditioner put both liquid products in one bottle in order to make hair washing and rinsing so much simpler, she gave me that same smirk and headshake. More recently, I wondered aloud if the asphalt roads in America could be layered with rubber products like ground-up and liquefied used tires. In this way, the drive would be smoother with rubber tires gliding over smooth rubber roads. This would also eliminate the potholes that result in jarring car rides.

"You're so funny," she answered with the usual smirk and eye-roll emphasizing her mocking facial expression. Now the "You're so funny" remark can be applied to the guys and gals encountered on golf courses all over the country. The persons you will be discovering in these pages are real, and the events surrounding them are also real. In golf, as with life, you can't make this stuff up.

Thank you Zoey, Sarah, and Carol for being so honest and direct. Your comments and assistance have helped me dog paddle my way through this tidal wave of cynicism.

According to a study in a Scandinavian medical journal, golfers live five years longer than non-players, and the lower your handicap, the longer you live. We all hope this is true, and be sure to remind our bowling buddies of this research and how we will outlive them. Someday my golf score might beat my age, assuming, of course, I live to be one hundred, which coincidently happens to be my bowling average, too.

And one more advantage to the game… err… "sport" of golf— The more rounds played, the better our chances of meeting more Characters on the Green.

CHAPTER 1

Family and Friends

ALTHOUGH MY WIFE of thirty-six years is a non-golfer, I have shaped her into a great golf watcher, as she enjoys (or more appropriately, tolerates) watching the pro golfers on TV. Carol first became faintly interested in golf in 1981 when we walked the Sea Pines Championship Course at the Heritage Golf Classic on Hilton Head Island, South Carolina. On a clear, warm April day filled with brilliant sunshine and blue skies with wispy clouds of a creamy marshmallow texture, we followed the players.

On one par-3 hole, we stood directly behind three professionals. It was a Wednesday, a practice day, and I stood observing their stances and swings from close range. Tom Watson, Bob Murphy, and Hubert Green were on the tee while we stood behind the rope just a few feet away, with no one else nearby. I was mostly interested in their technique; Carol more interested in the golf fashion of the day. All three pros turned and talked to us, asked where we were from, and said, "Thanks for watching." Congenial Bob Murphy, who upon seeing that Carol was seven months pregnant, patted her on the stomach and remarked, "So you were in the right place at the wrong time!" Tom Watson then addressed Murphy with his chubby, rotund physique and mid-sized beer belly. "And what is your excuse, Murph?" he said as he patted Murphy's stomach. Tom Watson has remained Carol's favorite pro to this day.

Carol watches golf on TV with or without me in the living room. And that's because she has to—the *Golf Channel* is always on as mandatory viewing. But many mornings she will inquire if a tournament is on and where it is being held. Her favorite, our favorite, is the one at Pebble Beach every February. The course extends into the ocean or perhaps the ocean permeates the course, sea birds forever hovering and swooping, squawking in the misty sky, warning of danger below. They're probably screeching in bird-talk that it is *their* territory, where ocean, sand, and rocks collide. The cliffs are treacherous, and the ocean, a shanked shot off the raised fairways, reaches skyward to swallow any manmade object hurled in its direction.

Carol wants to go there to feel it in person. She actually *wants* to see the tournament, see Pebble Beach, and hang around with the celebrities. Especially Ray Romano, who she can't believe is a golfer, and who she has seen play on television in the Wednesday Pro-Am. Romano, of comedy and TV fame from *Everybody Loves Raymond*, could easily be the subject of a chapter in this book. But the characters in this book are your everyday guys, unique and quirky in their own right, even though they try not to be. Sometimes being a famous celebrity has its drawbacks, such as not being able to star in my book. But as the show reminds us, everybody loves you anyway, Raymond.

My personal favorite to watch is, of course, *The Masters*, which kicks off in early April from Augusta, Georgia. Having watched a round and walked along many of the holes in person, I can say that the TV cameras do it no justice at all. It's a sight I'll never forget. The course is nowhere near flat—the greens are severely sloped. And the grounds are immaculate. Pink, lavender, and red azaleas engulf you, and the fragrance of sweet air-filled cologne waits at every bend. The white-pinkish hue emanating from the dogwood trees is nearly as flawless as a multicolored canvas painting. The grass is greener than green. If I were a TV executive, I'd attempt to capture the uniqueness and beauty of the surroundings in several more captivating ways.

First, I'd place remote cameras about ten feet off the ground within the trees, above the gallery view. With this new perspective, TV viewers would be able to watch the players climbing the hills and would have a better angle, seeing if the course sloped upward or downward. Next, I would put "hat cameras" on the standard bearers, the folks who walk around with the signs displaying the golfers' names and current scores. The standard bearers are close enough to the action but far enough away so that they don't disturb the pro making the shot. I'd call this technology the "Hatcam." Lastly, can we get a ground view of the putting surface, please? A small camera at golf ball level at selected holes would easily be unobtrusive. The golfer won't see it, but the viewers would get an interesting perspective of how the pro lines up to visualize his putt. For this idea, I'd attach a camera to the near bottom of a moveable stick, about a foot above ground level. Any cameraman, or volunteer, or trained monkey could move the camera-stick to the appropriate place prior to putts attempted.

Because I am now tech-savvy, I'm aware that all of these ideas are within reach and doable. Smarter tech geeks can figure this out, and not only for the Masters, but for most of the PGA and LPGA tournaments all year long. Hey—at least this time I didn't get the "You're so funny" comment and facial smirk from Carol.

Television producers and directors need to realize that showing a golf ball in midair flight is veryyyyyyyyyyyy booooooooring and sooooooo Seventies technology. We'd rather see Tiger, Phil, or Rory react to their errant shots from the ground view than watch the golf ball in midair. Who cares about a ball flying through the air? Watching any pro kick the ground, pound the ground with his club in disgust, and shove the club back into his bag is much more entertaining than watching the ball fly through the air.

C'mon, this is what competitors do in the heat of the moment. Whether right or wrong, don't judge and analyze their behavior on national TV. This type of behavior makes amateurs feel closer to the pro level, to see pros as real people. Everyone remembers Sergio Garcia at a younger age running up the fairway and kicking his heels after making a terrific, miraculous recovery shot at the 1999 PGA Championship. The ground camera crew recorded this action and it was memorable. Not the ball's flight, but Sergio's reaction. Good stuff. And to see Bubba Watson's unbelievable save out of the woods at the Masters playoff hole in 2012 was exciting. The cameraman had a great view of Bubba chopping out of danger in the woods, and the ensuing bounce in his step back to the green. Hey, haven't we all been in the woods trying to hack out of trouble and back into play? Well, some of us more often than others but, to the point, it was exciting to see Bubba in that predicament.

Carol and I made a trip to the Ryder Cup in 2012 at the Medina Country Club near Chicago. Had to do it—the Ryder Cup is a must-see event for all golfers. Better than attending the Super Bowl, although I like football, and it's a lot less expensive too. Our friend, another Patrick, accompanied us for the weekend. Patrick is a youthful, energetic, excitable golf nut who loves the competitive spirit of the game. To him, it is not just a game—it is asserting one's superiority and dominance over the opponent. He does not like to lose.

Following Saturday's round, the American team was way ahead by six points, a nearly insurmountable advantage leading into the Sunday singles matches. We definitely had an influence on the Saturday matches in our red, white, and blue-colored shirts, encouraging the Americans by shouting in unison "U-S-A, U-S-A" whenever necessary. But the American team lost on Sunday, which gave way to Patrick screaming and cussing as the Europeans sank putt after putt on that final day. Years later he is still upset that the Ryder Cup went to the Euros. As I said, he does not like to lose.

My wife has accompanied me on the golf course several times throughout the years, even though she doesn't play. She has enjoyed the outdoors, the calmness of the surroundings, the beauty of the grounds, and the chance to take a ride in the cart and read a book. These days she encourages me to play several times each week as a ploy to get me out of the house. There was a time that I nearly lost that privilege.

A friend of ours, Rick, joined us for a round at Kingsmill Resort on a warm and muggy summer day in Williamsburg, southeastern Virginia. Clouds were forming off the nearby

James River, but we didn't think much of it, shrugging it off as a typical summer day. With just the two of us golfing, the starter added a third guy to our group and, because Carol was in her own cart, she rode along with the stranger. He seemed harmless, a decent golfer—no way of knowing if he was an ax-murdering serial killer or Mr. Nice Guy. As we approached the third hole, we suddenly heard thunder in the distance and could see lightning through the thickening clouds about fifteen miles to our southwest. I knew storms were known to form here as they followed the path of the James River that meandered along Williamsburg and Kingsmill's aptly named "River Course." Rick Donaldson, an active duty Army Specialist, and myself, a former Army Infantry Officer, used the Army's "flash to bang" time in estimating the distance of the approaching storm. This formula was taught during the Cold War years for the purpose of determining distances of nuclear detonations in the open field of battle, so why not for our thunderstorm situation on the course?

As we walked off the third green, it started raining, unforgiving and unrelenting pelts of rain. The lightning and thunder were both visible and loud, so we prudently decided to stop playing. Rick and I scooted off in our cart toward the next tee, where the cart path entered a tunnel under the main entrance road leading to the clubhouse. There it was dry and away from any danger of lightning; a perfect place to wait out the passing storm. Except it didn't pass quickly, and it came upon us much sooner than we estimated. I guess the "flash to bang" equation only really works for nuclear explosions, in theory. Thank God we never had to find out on the battlefield.

We were safe, away from any danger, but where in thunder was Carol and our stranger? They didn't know the course as Rick and I did, and they didn't see us scoot away down the cart path through the gray mist, sideways rain, and rumbling low clouds. We assumed they had retreated back to the club-house through the pouring rain to safety. Again, wrong answer. We forgot the Army's response to nearly everything in a soldier's life—"Never assume anything." The storm eventually passed, but it continued to drip heavy droplets of rain, making the rest of the round unplayable considering the rain-soaked sogginess of the playing conditions.

As we headed back to the clubhouse, retracing back through holes three and two, we uncovered the whereabouts of our playing companion and Carol, the rider. They had decided that hiding under a tall oak tree was favorable to driving through the downpour. But lightning, heavy rain, and a big oak tree are not a good combination, especially if the surrounding terrain nearby is relatively flat and open. At least the guy wasn't a serial killer, and Carol was alive. Soaked down to the skin, with flattened hair and water filling her shoes, she was not happy to see us, especially when I offered her my golf umbrella. It got worse when we realized that her open purse had been sitting in the exposed basket behind the cart's seat. It was completely filled with water. Her driver's license, credit card, dollar bills, and lipstick tube were floating around like peaceful ducks on a small tranquil pond.

Rick and I still had the itch to play some holes, and seeing that the skies were clear and blue again, we asked Carol to drop us off at the Fort Eustis golf course, about fifteen miles away as the crow flies, where it did not rain a single drop all day.

"Enjoy your golf, boys," she muttered as she maliciously drove off with tires squealing, kicking up loose gravel, pebbles, and dirty projectiles that rained against our clubs, bags, and bodies.

Some years later, I volunteered at the PGA Championship at Oak Hill Country Club in Rochester, New York. In August of that year, my sister, Anne, and her longtime friend, Linda, accompanied me on the Wednesday practice day. My companions had never been to a professional golf tournament, but I guaranteed it would be an opportunity of a lifetime. Even more exciting for the novices would be to obtain as many autographs of the pros as possible and to see them in person during their practice routines. This I also guaranteed. Clutching their souvenir PGA flags, they set out to accomplish this mission. It was my first day on the job as volunteer marshal on the opening hole, therefore their mission was most important for me since my day was occupied with crowd control, public relations, assisting patrons, observing golfers' ball trajectory and landings, and a full day's worth of marshaling.

On the road to the course parking area, there were several young enterprising entrepreneurs selling unused tickets for the day's event. As the hawkers held up their tickets for the passersby to see, Linda the Liberal remarked, "They should have a sign with the prices listed so more people will be interested in buying them."

"I don't think so—they're trying to get whatever they can for the tickets. It's called bartering," I dryly replied.

"How does anyone know how much they're selling them for?" she asked.

"They have to ask, naturally."

"A set, advertised price is better," my Upstate New York Ultra-Liberal friend tried to explain.

Anne, a former high school American History teacher, attempted to give us a historical perspective. "And you'd make buyers pay federal and New York State taxes on top of that, not to mention local and county taxes, too. So, the sign might read, 'Tickets, twenty dollars each plus tax,' so the cost of the ticket would be thirty dollars, a third more than advertised. Nobody wants to pay that. The guy is trying to make a buck—it's called the free enterprise system. This is a long-standing tradition in the U.S."

She continued, "Native American Indians introduced the sport of Lacrosse to the white settlers. In order to fund these games and to make ends meet, the Native Americans allowed settlers entry into the games in exchange for blankets, beads, and trinkets. Entrepreneurial Indians scalped their tickets to the highest bidders who offered the most items. Everybody walked away happy, without government interference."

"The Chief later realized they got the bad end of this deal," I contributed, "but they got their revenge by landing a professional football team out in Kansas City and a professional baseball team in Cleveland."

By the way, has anyone ever asked the Native American Indians what name they prefer? With so much controversy surrounding the politically correct name for Native American,

I decided to ask. It wasn't a scientific experiment or an authorized opinion poll; I merely asked some Native American-looking guys how they felt. Their answers may astound you. They told me that they preferred to be identified on the basis of their original tribe—"Cherokee," "Pamunkey," "Mohawk," "Seminole," and so on—their founding origins. They didn't much care about the terms "Native American" or "Indian" at all. Makes perfect sense as most people are proud of their ancestral heritage.

Linda, the Liberal, and Anne, enjoyed their one-and-only time at a major professional golf tournament. They garnered twenty autographs between the two of them and walked away with some unusual memories. Only problem was that neither woman knew any of the golfers whose autographs they'd received. Thanks to the signatures being signed expeditiously and the signers having unrecognizable flares to their autographs, we spent the next four days in deciphering mode.

"Hmmm, this guy was wearing a blue-striped shirt with gray trousers and a hat that said 'Titleist' scribbled across the front. This guy had a green shirt that didn't match his pants. One of the players was chubby, kinda fat around the waist, but was very nice to everyone."

Oh, these were great descriptions, but names would've helped. I needed Inspector Clouseau and all the detectives from *Law and Order* for this caper.

How I became a marshal for hole #1 at the Oak Hill Country Club remains a mystery. Hole #1 duties were reserved for "members only" of that exclusive club. Not a member, nor exclusive, I signed up on the volunteer website anyway. The mistake was innocent and probably an honest oversight by the PGA. Answering truthfully, when asked if I was a member, I checked the "yes" block, thinking the question pertained to membership with the PGA. Associate Members were included; I was ninety percent positive about that. Maybe it was my past experiences or just plain good looks that landed me the position. Or maybe the committee was desperate for helpers. But, I later discovered that all of the other marshals that week were Oak Hill Club members. Some of the scornful glances that I received from the actual members were Hall of Fame-worthy, too.

It didn't matter in the end because the week was an immeasurable success for the tournament.

I also worked as a volunteer the previous year at the PGA held on Kiawah Island, South Carolina. During both tournaments, I served as a hole marshal volunteer, giving me first-hand experience of the differences between New Yawkers and Southerners regarding golf course supervisory styles.

In New York, the volunteer captain required us to meet thirty minutes before the start of the shift. Behind the grandstand he took attendance as he blared out names like an Army Drill Sergeant. At Kiawah in South Carolina, we met fifteen minutes before the start of our shift under a huge cypress tree with hanging moss near the ninth green. The volunteer captain greeted us by name with a smile and said, "Glad you can help out."

In New York, we were directed to our position around the hole and informed to "Go right now." In South Carolina we were asked our preference of position and told to "Get there when you can."

In New York, a slip of paper was passed from one volunteer to the next as we switched positions every thirty minutes. The theory was that the paper would circulate back to the captain once everyone had shifted around the entire hole. In South Carolina, the captain came around to say, "How y'all doin?" and "Time to shift positions."

In South Carolina, we were continually asked if we needed sunscreen. It was August and hot. In New York, no mention of sunscreen. It was August and hot.

In South Carolina, I was able to remain at the teeing area or the greenside area for the entire four hours of the shift. These were great viewing areas for both fans and marshals. In New York, only the "Oak Hill Members" and those who were buddies with the captain got those assignments.

In New York, I was repeatedly questioned, "How did you manage to get on hole #1? Isn't this for members only? Are you a member?"

In South Carolina, I heard, "You have a great location. We know you're enjoying it."

In South Carolina, my hole was #9, which stretched alongside the Atlantic Ocean. Between the ocean and fairway were the beach and sand dunes. Each day the wind whipped off the ocean, sandblasting me from head to toe. Sand stuck to my sunscreen-coated body. I felt like I had been rolled through the beach and covered in sand like a sprinkle-covered ice cream cone. In New York, hole #1 was lined with majestic oaks, allowing for plenty of shade. The thick, green, lush grass made me feel like I was on a summer picnic. The breezes had a cooling effect, and I only felt hot after hearing a local say, "Hot enough for ya, but whadyagonna do? I'm just sayin'."

In South Carolina, the volunteer hospitality tent was located conveniently nearby. Folks served lunches and drinks in the large air-conditioned tent, which offered a place to sit, relax, and cool off. In New York, there wasn't a volunteer hospitality tent in sight. If there was a tent, then it was somewhere way off the fifteenth fairway.

In New York, the volunteer parking area was combined with the public parking area in a huge space once owned by Kodak, the film and camera company. The factories were closed and empty, but parking was abundant. It was located off the main interstate, easily accessible from all directions. In South Carolina, volunteers parked in a separate farmer's field closed to the general public. The entry was fifteen miles down a mostly two-lane back road with moss-covered trees hugging each side of the road. One way in and one way out. It felt a little spooky after dark, with the wispy moss branches forming menacing shapes, waving in concert with the nighttime summer breezes, forewarning the coming of the Headless Horseman from out of the fields.

Yes, there were stark differences between Northerners and Southerners and in the way they personally interacted. Work was conducted in two distinct ways, yet both events were successful. Each situation was a unique experience and were downright fun-filled days inside the tournament ropes.

CHAPTER **2**

Tournament People

THE BEST WAY to attend a professional golf tournament is to volunteer. Volunteers get to be near the action, the golfers, and the live events around the course. The only hindrance is that you actually have to *work* for three or four days. For the men's Anheuser-Busch tournament at the Kingsmill Resort some years ago, I volunteered to play security guard. Yes—the very same River Course that nearly caused my stormy divorce was played by the pros. The Anheuser-Busch was played in the heat and humidity of July in Williamsburg, Virginia. That particular year the temperature seemed to climb to about 180 degrees, according to my internal thermometer, accounting, of course, for the humidity too. "It's not the heat, but that humidity," the locals said. Whatever it was, it was still a Pakistani-type of heat that could melt hard-shell M&Ms inside and out.

We security guards were dressed fashionably by a professional security company. Guards were issued military-style heavy-duty polyester pants, dark blue with a wide white stripe down the length of the legs. We were also each given a long-sleeved heavy cotton white gabardine dress shirt with a button-down collar that kept the matching navy blue necktie in place. Completing the ensemble was a bright fire-engine red woolen sports jacket. Some of the security jobs consisted of directing tournament traffic on the hot summer melting asphalt, patrolling the exclusive parking areas where the pros or their drivers parked for them and other VIPs, like the mayor and governor, or guarding the entrance to the forbidden clubhouse and golfers' locker room, off limits to spectators. As explained by the Tournament Director and the head security guard, they were "all very important positions." Not explained was that the issued uniform weighed a mere eighteen pounds. With sweat dripping from pores like a leaky faucet, a guard could expect to lose up to twenty pounds each day during his six hour shift, unless he passed out first, which was my plan if chosen to support one of those "very important positions." At least I'd look good, really sharp and professional, while crashing to the pavement.

Due to my military experience, background, and highly regarded intelligence, my assignment was to guard the *indoor* buffet food arrangement. Aaaah, inside with air-conditioning, a comfortable 72 degrees. The daylong buffet offered a spread of freshly baked pastries, bagels, fresh fruit, tiny sandwiches, nuts, pretzels, water, soda, coffee, tea, beer (Budweiser, of course), and other assorted non-alcoholic drinks. All inside a fairly large banquet room set up for the golfers, who wandered in and out during the tournament. Other VIPs were allowed to enter as long as we could clearly see the credentials that they carried on ribbons around their necks.

Such a high level, top-secret mission required two dedicated and experienced guards: myself and Gus, who became my mentor for the week. A gentleman of around seventy-five, Gus was a longtime fixture at this prestigious location. We were allowed one chair outside the door entrance to the buffet banquet room so that we could alternate sitting during our shift. Gus, the most senior member of the entire security force, was given the honor of remaining seated during our time together, which he did not relinquish for five days. I learned a lot from Gus.

The three most important General Guard Orders taught by the military soon became useful for Gus and me. The first, "I will not leave my post until properly relieved." The second, "I will follow orders of my superiors to the best of my ability." And the third, "I will walk my post from flank to flank and take no shit from any rank." I am paraphrasing the third, but my version is better than the original.

Gus took his security position very, very seriously, checking each visitor for the proper credentials. Or at least he did when he was awake. I was tasked with double duty: checking for credentials and checking to see when Gus was awake, the hardest part of the job. He expected me to pace the hallway leading to the banquet room, back and forth like the guards in the movie *Stalag 17*, or the TV show *Hogan's Heroes*. I never should have told him I was a military veteran and was not surprised when he asked me to "low crawl" to assume a better advantaged security position. In the Army it is called "minimal defilade," to lower your height profile so as not to be seen from afar by opposing forces. Because there was nowhere to properly hide, I just crouched low behind the buffet food tables.

We managed to see some of the golf being played on the course thanks to the two big screen TVs in the room we were guarding. And we met several pro golfers as they entered to enjoy the food and drinks. I doubt if the other guards outside were able to experience any of this, but at least they were losing some weight without having to diet—yet another benefit of volunteering.

Years later, the LPGA began using the Kingsmill Resort and the River Course for one of their tournament stops in early May. This time I was assigned to help out on the driving range with other active duty and retired military members. This was going to be real close to the action, so it'd be entertaining to see the professionals as they practiced before and after their play. It was a dream job—working out in the fresh air thanks to the lower spring-like temperatures and wearing a casual moisture-wicking polo shirt and khaki shorts. No heavy uniform and necktie.

The military person in charge of the overall operation of the driving range was an active duty Navy Command Master Chief. His regular Navy job was "Chief of the Boat," the highest-ranking enlisted person on a Navy submarine and a very highly-respected position. The "Chief" carries out the orders of the Commander and helps to ensure that all logistics, tactics, and strategies are fulfilled when underway under the ocean waters. Although this Chief's background and supervisory experiences seemed quite appropriate for this less-complicated landlubber mission, he was more of a pain in the ass than a leader. He gave orders such as "full speed ahead," "prepare to launch," and "secure the range for use," and expected us to respond with "aye, aye, Chief." He placed maps of the course, driving range, and surrounding grounds area in the "command center"—the nearby dilapidated, yet functional, trailer that was used as a break area for volunteers. He wrote color-coded notes on the map stapled to the bulletin board to denote specific responsibilities, such as picking up range balls. He also identified the location of washing areas and latrines, or rather, the "head" in Navy talk, as well as cart path locations, or "escape and evasion routes." And he outlined several emergency responses in the case of "encountering shallow water," or *rain*, as civilians call it.

Any good military organization on a mission will ensure that a steady supply of coffee is available for its troops. And, indeed, the Chief had a coffeemaker as well as a personnel roster to ensure that fresh coffee would always be available throughout the day. Leading by example as described in Leadership 101, he'd always have a fresh coffee cup in hand while barking orders. Drinking coffee and delegating duties were his two primary tasks. He had turned the break area trailer into his own personal dry dock submarine. I miss Gus already.

The driving range, where my station was to be, was a short distance from the "command trailer." I followed the thin red line on the command post strategic map, which outlined the cart path to my destination. Several volunteers were assisting the golfers and caddies as they approached the driving range to practice and warm up prior to their tee time. Golf balls, which had been hit down range, were gathered by the picker and dumped into the giant ball-washing machine. These golf balls were delivered to us in fifty-five gallon plastic tubs. We sorted these clean golf balls into three brand categories:

Titleist, Callaway, and Nike, and hand-dried each with a bath towel. This activity was reminiscent of a scene from the *I Love Lucy* TV series—the one in which Lucy and Ethel work in a chocolate factory sorting and separating manufactured candies as they pass by on a conveyor belt. Thank goodness we didn't have to eat the golf balls like the chocolates that Lucy and Ethel ate.

We then placed each of the dry balls in separate, smaller buckets for the pros to use. Professional golfers are fanatics when it comes to the brand of golf ball they use. Some golfers are only willing to use one particular brand, while some must obey written contracts with golf ball manufacturers, ensuring the mandatory use of a particular brand.

Many of the golfers were recognizable to us, so we slipped their names on their signboards and placed them near their practice areas. The teeing area was raised about twenty feet from the path leading up to it so that the golfers needed to ascend ten steps to the level ground as they approached. The range supervisor, Frank, another volunteer and member of the Kingsmill Resort, positioned himself at the bottom of the steps in order to give us advance notice of the approaching golfers. Most of the female golfers had their name embossed somewhere on their golf bag, usually on the side, but sometimes on the very bottom. Frank, always clever and inconspicuous as possible, searched for the names of the few golfers he didn't recognize. Frank could have been a CIA or FBI field agent in the way that he used secretive stealth measures to identify each golfer—it seemed quite possible that this was an early form of "profiling" later adopted by the FBI. His method seemed to be working quite well, but there was one unforeseen problem.

Many nationalities are represented in the world of golf, with a good number of golfers hailing from Asian countries. South Korea is one country well represented by many excellent players, several of whom share the same surname, such as Kim or Pak. More than half the population has the name Kim and the other forty percent has the name of Pak. Or so it seems. Probably not statistically accurate—you'd have to ask Judy McElroy, the statistician lady. I can attest to this fact after working in YongSan, South Korea for a year. There were two civilian secretaries in the office named Ms. Pak, and two government local national workers named Mr. Kim. In an adjoining office we had Ms. Pak and Mr. Pak, though not related. I also got to know another Mr. Kim quite well, the starter at the military golf course. Despite not understanding the difficult Hangul language, knowing the two names Kim and Pak made personal introductions and interactions much easier during my time in that country. I had a fifty percent chance of guessing the correct name when meeting strangers.

On the LPGA tour, there were a few rising stars named Kim. The American, Christina Kim, originally from California, was most recognizable. There were at least six others with Korean names in the tournament. After four of them had practiced that day, just two remained. Unfortunately for Frank, he was unable to find any names on the two remaining bags carried by the caddies. With a fifty percent chance of being right and a fifty percent chance of being wrong, Frank decided to take a gamble. After realizing that the wrong "Kim" had been added to the signboard, her followers, and especially her caddy, accused the volunteers of creating a character assassination of international magnitude. Our unfortunate debacle of misnaming the proper Kim was offensive to the Koreans. We were guilty of defamation, according to the onlookers. Her caddy declared that all of us should be fired immediately.

The Chief, made aware of the situation, spoke up. "No—only Frank should be fired, not everybody."

Can volunteers really be fired from volunteering? And fired over one unfortunate mistake? Nah, and besides, Frank was best suited for the job. After receiving lengthy apologies, Ms. Kim and her caddy were satisfied. I like to think I helped when I asked the caddy, "Have you ever made an honest mistake?" He walked away grumbling something in his native Hangul language filled with guttural, grunting sounds. I'm sure it was, "Okay, you crazy American, just wait until I tell Mr. Pak what happened here."

The LPGA does things the right way, administratively speaking, in regard to encouraging the local community to support the event. At the LPGA Kingsmill Championship, thirteen hundred volunteers are recruited to help out during the week. On weekends, teenagers get the opportunity to participate as youth Standard Bearers. These kids, strong and energetic, tend to be local high school students who play on their school golf teams or freshmen and sophomores in college vying for a position on their school teams—with one exception, that is.

My granddaughter, Zoey, wanted to volunteer to see the "Pink Panther," Paula Creamer, play in the tournament. So I signed her up, filling out her birth date and all other relevant information. She ended up landing the very last volunteer opening for the weekend. At nine years old and four feet tall, she was the youngest, most petite volunteer on the course. The sign pole to the standard was taller than she was. When the

Tournament Supervisor asked if she thought she could carry such a large sign, her answer was modest and childlike, "Yes. I can lift my mommy up." Laughter all around. She got the gig for that Saturday and Sunday.

She manned the first tee, nervously awaiting her first-ever walk down the fairway with the pros. The pros started by introducing themselves to the volunteers. First was Lexi Thompson, followed by Brittany Lang and Azahara Munoz. Not a bad first pairing for an impressionable youngster. The young ladies were kind, welcoming, and genuinely interested in meeting the helpers. The men of the PGA could learn from such behavior. Not to suggest that the PGA players weren't cordial, but the women took a special interest in the youngsters around them.

At the end of the round, each golfer handed Zoey an autographed golf ball. They called her back into the scoring tent where Ms. Munoz gave her a big hug and told her, "Zoey, you are my favorite." Maybe her birdie on the treacherous eighteenth influenced the thought. It certainly didn't hurt.

On day two, coincidently, Christina Kim and Azahara Munoz were paired up. Upon seeing my beaming little granddaughter, Ms. Munoz again enveloped her in a big hug and announced, "Zoey, I'm so glad you are with me again." Whispers went up in the crowd surrounding the tee. Who was this lucky leprechaun in the oversized neon green shirt and floppy hat that covered her eyes and forehead?

Maybe Zoey was a lucky charm for these players that weekend. Lexi Thompson finished second, Brittany Lang finished fifth (after being in contention), and Christina Kim and

Azahara Munoz both finished in the top ten. Unfortunately, "Pink Panther" Paula Creamer did not make the cut for this tournament—very rare for her at Kingsmill. She must have had the wrong kids carrying her sign and score. No lucky little munchkin for her. Zoey still likes Ms. Creamer, but her newest favorite is Azahara Munoz, who, after all, has "that cool half-Spanish, half-English accent."

Another PGA tour location is the Honda Classic in southern Florida, where I took a buddies trip and tamed the Bear Trap with two friends, "Air Force Patrick" and "Scottso." We didn't actually play the National's Championship Course that hosts the Honda Classic in Palm Gardens, but we did observe holes #15, #16, and #17 on the final day of the Honda. This is the three-hole gauntlet that encompasses the famous Bear Trap that the pros must master in order to have a chance at winning the tournament.

"It's not about length," said Jack Nicklaus, the golf legend who designed the holes. "It's about precision and guts."

The heck it isn't about length! Jack doesn't know what he's talking about, with all due respect. "He don't know Jack," I say. After merely walking the cart path outside the ropes along the edges of these three holes, my companions and I had to pause for short rests and to suck in more oxygen. It was a breezy, sun drenched, 80-degree afternoon, and we hadn't even had to walk the previous fourteen holes leading to the Bear Trap.

Hole #15 is a 179-yard par 3, and it's a bear alright. The view from the tee box gets guys nervous. The fact that it's water short, right, and long makes the green seem even smaller than it is, especially if there's wind. Nerves cause tension, which restricts muscle movement. This leads to shorter, quicker swings that produce errant shots. Ever played in a local two-man or four-man scramble tournament? Then you know the feeling.

Hole #16 is just 434 yards, and a par 4; *just* 434 yards, where a solid drive up the fairway leaves an uphill approach over water and sand, two of the most dreaded elements for amateurs and another classic anxiety-inducing stressor. At the corner of the dogleg right, we rested in some shade under a waving palm tree to watch the pros agonize over their approach shots to the green. George Mackenzie's caddy passed us, giving us a nod and a brief wave as if to say, "Nice to see you, my guy is doing well." And, yes, he was two-under at the time.

Mackenzie's caddy happened to be staying at the same hotel as we were in West Palm Beach. Earlier that morning he noticed us three "touristas" flunking our course in photography outside the hotel and offered to take our picture, the mandatory poolside-by-the-palm-tree picture of southern Florida. For a second or two I thought he might zoom off with my camera, since he was sitting in the driver's seat of his rented car. And with his seemingly phony Australian accent, I figured he was a caddy in the same way that I was a caddy. In reality, he was Mackenzie's actual caddy, and a true gentleman, as far as we could tell. Thanks for the picture and a good memory, Mate!

At that same shady corner of the dogleg on hole #16, we spotted a young man in a Cubs baseball cap also watching the action, puffing on a big aromatic stogie. Jason was working on a Macanudo cigar; I actually smelled him before seeing him. Macanudos are fine cigars handmade in Nicaragua by professional tobacco rollers. Cigars are only aromatic if you enjoy the smell of finely hand-rolled tobacco smoke curling through the air. They stink if you don't. It's a matter of preference, I suppose, like plaid pants from the Seventies. I've kept my plaid green and white polyester pants in recognition of the fact that they are slowly starting to make a fashion comeback. Tell my wife. Maybe you, too, will experience the eye roll, smirk, and headshake, and the "You're so funny" comment from her.

Macanudos are a somewhat expensive cigar, especially for a young enlisted military man in the Coast Guard such as Jason Dunlap. But this was a special occasion, as he would inform me. A native Chicagoan, he was currently stationed at the Fort Lauderdale Coast Guard Station. A Midwesterner from a landlocked state, now enjoying the southern coast near Miami. How does this happen? Do the military recruiters in the middle of the country use exotic-looking posters of tropical climates to lure potential recruits away from the heartland? And do the military recruiters on the coasts use posters of mountains, trees, and green fields to incite the imagination of shore-dwellers? Navy statistics do show that the majority of their sailors are in fact from the midsection of the country. Oh, those clever recruiters!

Jason noticed the brand of my cigar, H. Upmann, and offered a one-for-one exchange. Both the Macanudo and H. Upmann were of equal value and quality, so we gladly made the swap. "Air Force Patrick," a genuine Irishman himself, tipped me off to the fact that H. Upmann was the brand that the late President John F. Kennedy routinely smoked. Now there were three things that JFK and I had in common: cigar brand, chronically sore, stiff lower back, and experience running an important organization. Mine was a one hundred twenty-person Army Transportation Truck Company. Kennedy's position was a slightly larger organization comprised of around three hundred million people.

The final hole of the Bear Trap was a par 3, 190 yards. A hole such as #17 has an important lesson to teach amateurs—don't play it, skip right past it, and you'll feel better about your golf that day. But according to Mike Bender, Golf Magazine's Top 100 Teacher, whose students include PGA Tour stars Zach Johnson and Jonathan Byrd, "When playing in the wind, let the ball ride the breeze if you have room on the safe side." Safe side? What safe side exactly? "Here the prevailing wind is left to right and the water is to the green's right. Yes, there is a bunker left of the green, but that's certainly the better alternative," according to professor Bender. I guess that's a better alternative than clunking it into the mouth of the gator waiting on the opposite side of the green with his family and friends. Gators are everywhere, according to the Florida tourism experts and most locals, and you haven't experienced Florida golf unless you have encountered one on the golf course.

At the beautifully designed Arnold Palmer Legends Course at Orange Lake near Orlando, we saw several gators during our playing round, and my companions approached one that was lying stationary on the bank of a swamp near the edge of the fairway at hole #14. Danny had his seven-year-old son, Mason, along for the ride on the back nine, and in his attempt to impress the boy, he cautiously approached the twelve-foot long monster and tossed a Titleist at him. That didn't quite do anything except bounce off the gator's rough, scaly back. The adrenaline kicked in when the youngster said, "Run over him, Dad." The oldest member of the trio, Mason's grandpa, Roy, thought this was a terrific idea and that it would "show that gator who's boss around here," and tell it to "get off my fairway." (Old people tend to talk a big game—mostly grandfathers, when their grandsons are involved.) Sanity was restored when the "drive-by" didn't work either. The gator hunkered as stoic as a granite gargoyle. Then Mason exclaimed, "Get out an' grab his tail." Thankfully grandpa ignored this last request as we drove onward to see and live through the next four holes.

It was at hole #17, at the Patriots' Outpost adjoining the final hole of the Bear Trap, where we met two of our nation's real-life military heroes. The Patriots' Outpost was sponsored by United Technologies, owners of Pratt & Whitney and Sirkorsky. This tent-covered area, running nearly the length of the left side of the seventeenth, was erected "to honor the men and women of the U.S. Armed Forces," as the ad read in the tournament brochure.

What an honor they bestowed on all active military, retired military and their immediate families! They provided a free lunch of hamburgers, hot dogs, potato salad, baked beans, cole slaw, green salad, bread, and dessert. Drinks were included. It was a superbly run "military operation" by employees of United Technologies and many volunteers.

After receiving our meal, we haplessly searched around for a place to sit in the very busy and crowded area. A young lady standing near an open table and several chairs, apparently guarding the location for someone, offered the seats to us.

"Oh, they aren't due back for a while, they went out to the picnic area," she said. The picnic area was located just outside the circus-sized tent, on a cleanly-manicured grassy area with umbrella-covered tables and seating, and a great view of the entire 190 yards of the seventeenth hole.

Sure enough, while I was in the middle of a spoonful of baked beans, the two former occupants came to reclaim their rightful seats and table. Eighty-seven-year-old Angelo Cona, Italian immigrant and World War II Marine Corps Veteran, came hobbling up to us with cane in hand. I could've sworn he was "The Godfather," the old and weathered Marlon Brando.

Angelo is a member of the "Greatest Generation," and it was clearly reasonable to see why. It was his duty, he said, to join the Marines and fight for our country after the attack on Pearl Harbor. He served in the Southeast Asia Pacific campaigns in 1945 and 1946. He was born in Italy in July of 1927 and moved to the United States in 1934. He lived in Brooklyn and entered the military in 1945. Stationed in China, he was assigned to watch over a group of prisoners. He remembers a day that he was giving orders to one of the prisoners, who seemed not to understand him. A higher-ranking officer came by, saw the commotion, and asked if he was having a problem. Angelo told him that the prisoner did not understand, but as the officer talked to him, he discovered that wasn't the case. Rather, because Corporal Cona was a lower rank, the Japanese prisoner refused to take orders from him. When Angelo introduced his two fellow Marines Mario and Guido to the prisoner, the prisoner could suddenly understand and follow orders. Mario and Guido were very persuasive Sicilians.

Immediately after the war's end, Angelo visited Pearl Harbor as it was being rebuilt after the bombing. Seeing all the destruction saddened him, but he also felt relieved that the war was over and that he wouldn't need to fight anymore. He spoke to me of a cousin who had died during the war who had his same exact name, Angelo Maria Cona.

After he was discharged he returned home and began working with his family for their landscaping business on Long Island, New York. He later got married, had two daughters, and joined the Deer Park volunteer fire department, eventually working his way up to chief. In 1995, he retired to Florida. These days he plays golf two times a week, bowls and plays cards weekly, and works around the yard. At eighty-seven he is still active, even after recently getting a pacemaker and needing a cane to hobble around.

Despite our age difference of roughly twenty-five years, our commonality was clear to me. Basic military training, harsh conditions, meal rations, uncomfortable uniforms and personal appearance standards, obedience, leadership, and pride in our military were the themes of the afternoon. Always a gentleman, Angelo said to me in his heavy accent, "I tuuurely enjoyed da' day, capice?"

While listening to Angelo's stories, Angelo's daughter, JoAnn, and son-in-law, Dave, introduced me to one of his buddies, John Illuzzi. John, originally from Rhode Island, was a Korean War veteran with the 15th Ranger Company (Airborne). With overwhelming spunk and energy, he declared, "You can look it up, I'm in there!" And so I did. Sure enough, Sergeant John Illuzzi single-handedly defeated the North Korean and Chinese Communists battle after battle, pushing them northward to the 38th parallel, where the Korean Demilitarized Zone (DMZ) remains to this day. John is a former soldier who you'd want on your side even today. He is lean, formidable and still feisty in his late seventies.

Both of these old timers still enjoy playing golf at their home course in the West Palm Beach region. They play for the fun of it, enjoying each other's company and retelling war stories. And it's a good bet that these two combat veterans make side wagers on every hole, whether the Marines or Army will win.

The Patriots' Outpost was a real treat and tribute to all of the military veterans and families who entered.

The Honda Classic is played in late February of each year. Later in the golfing season during June, ending on Fathers' Day, is the traditional U.S. Open. At the 2014 Men's U.S. Open, I met my two stepsisters for the first time. At least that's what I called them.

Marilyn Kidd and Carolyn Ashby, identical twins in their late fifties, had recently retired with over fifty years of combined school teaching experience. That's a lot of lesson plans and homework to cover. Marilyn, from the Washington D.C. area, and Carolyn, from Williamsport, Pennsylvania, were my volunteer partners and "stepsisters" for the week. Before arriving at their assignments in the afternoon, they had walked four and a half miles through the streets of Southern Pines, near Pinehurst, North Carolina. They were in perpetual motion, literally marching in place for the entire four hours of our credential-checking at the Members' Clubhouse. They stepped to their own mental music, as if they were both in need of a quick bathroom break. Their act was enough to impress an Army Drill Sergeant. I could practically hear the familiar bark, "Hut-two-three-four; get in step, you maggot!" Their arms were swinging, their legs were high stepping, and I was getting fatigued just watching them. My eyes jogged ten miles that day, trying to keep up the pace.

At the end of the day, the fitness apps on their smartphones announced a robust 32,368 steps taken for Marilyn and just 26,525 for Carolyn. Clearly she needed to pick up the pace. Holy Motion Sickness, Batman! Their routine covered more than six miles, including at least two miles stomping in one spot. And it's not that they needed to burn that many calories (I'd guess they were hitting eighteen thousand per day), as they were both in decent physical condition. Not chubby, not heavyset or even "big-boned," as mom would have us believe. Certainly not two of the millions of Americans who are over-weight or a third of the American adults who are described as obese by the American Health Association. How could they be, anyway? They didn't even stop for a second to eat.

All of this got me thinking of a way to help overweight and obese people, who clearly need a nudge to lose weight. Forget the exercise, not gonna start doing that, even though this plan would jumpstart the weight reduction. No, not the typical advice to eat less, eat more fruits and veggies, and drink more water. None of the stuff that nutritionists harp on again and again, nearly sounding like Charlie Brown's unseen classroom teacher: "Wa-wa, wa-wa."

While guarding the clubhouse, Carolyn, Marilyn, and I de-vised a simple, yet effective, plan for weight reduction management in the USA. Consider that most adults in the country, ninety-seven percent by the Automobile Association count, own a driver's license. This is equivalent to three hundred million drivers, give or take a few million, anyone over fifteen years old. If half are overweight, then that amounts to one hundred fifty million people. Driver's licenses are renewable at the state level every five years. But how does this tie into our plan? Simple. When it is your turn to renew, you must step on a calibrated scale at the local DMV office. Using the American Health Association guidelines for healthy weight, prescribed by the Director of Health and Human Services, your weight must fall into the acceptable range of the chart. An allowance of ten percent over or under the range is permitted in every case. If your weight falls outside the acceptance, then here comes the "wow factor," a penalty or surcharge is added to your driver's license registration renewal bill. This is *not* a tax, I'll tell my liberal, progressive friends. Instead it is an eco-minded, totally organic, "everybody should be healthy" reminder.

Consider a calorically-challenged person around the national average—twenty pounds over their allotted amount, including the ten percent overage. If the surcharge were five dollars per pound, then the income generated for the state would be one hundred dollars per person! Five dollars a pound is cheaper than the supermarket's average sirloin price, I remind both of my liberal friends. On the grand scale, one hundred fifty million renewals will produce in excess of seven hundred fifty million dollars each year, spread across the states. My stepsisters and I think this is a great way to provide extra income to the state's budgets and to lower the numbers of overweight people at the same time.

Drivers paying more for their licenses will definitely be incentivized to lose the pounds through another twist to the program—those exceeding the weight limit will have to renew in two years, rather than five years, putting them on the clock to shed the fat cells. The program will start twelve months in advance of the first year so that chubby folks can start preparing early. In five years of the upstart, we will see a trimmer, healthier America: lowered "bad" cholesterol levels—can't remember if it is the LDL or HDL kind—fewer cases of diabetes, fewer heart problems, healthier-looking skin and bodies, and many other benefits. On top of that, many more happy drivers who give you a wave and the right of way when you don't deserve it, and a thumbs up rather than the middle finger. Except in New Jersey. If you've ever driven the Turnpike there, you understand. All these exclusive benefits, thanks to our innovative "Driver of the Future" plan.

One person who could benefit from this brilliant plan is the guy who stood next to me down the first fairway, outside the ropes at the U.S. Open. He was all of maybe five foot eight and well over two hundred fifty pounds, judging by the girth of his beltline. His shaved head and scraggly grayish goatee and moustache made him a *Duck Dynasty* "Godwin" character look-alike. John Godwin is a funny guy whose commentary and quirky behavior I enjoy. This guy was not *him* but could have been.

As the golf balls flew past us, the un-Godwin gave his analysis. "Get down the middle—great shot," he said to no one in particular. I looked around to see if anyone was listening, but no one was. "Turn in, stay out of the rough. Man, he is good," came next. I said nothing, simply because of my "No

Chit-Chat Policy" that had been enacted on January 1. The power of my personal New Years' resolutions had come into play. I wanted to tell him, "It's not you, it's me, or rather it is the policy" but that also would have violated my policy. I walked away in silence as he continued on in the opposite direction, offering his instant analysis to the crowd and no one in particular.

As we contemplated our nationwide weight management concept, Marilyn, Carolyn, and I guarded the outside entrances to the Clubhouse, which overlooked the majestic first tee and the eighteenth green of Pinehurst Course #2. Our volunteer post was at the outside balcony entrance to the Legends corporate ballroom located upstairs in the Members' Clubhouse (MC) of the Pinehurst Country Club. The Clubhouse boasts a massive, recently renovated, pine-scented entryway that opens onto the infamous Donald Ross-designed monstrous golf course. Everything at Pinehurst is pine tree-scented. There are more pine trees on this golf property than there are people in all of North Carolina. Surrounding the nine course areas of the Pinehurst facility are neighboring towns named Southern Pines, Whispering Pines, Mid-Pines, Pine Needles, Tall Pines, and Pinetop, to name a few. This must be where the cleaning agent "Pine Sol" originated. As though the outside environment wasn't piney enough, they had to bring it inside the homes, too, pushing their sweet smelling, odorous pine scent onto kitchen counters, bathrooms, and hardwood floors. Southerners also rinse their hair with pine shampoo and pine conditioner after they have rolled around in the multitude of layers of pine straw that's scattered around every building in the Pine Barrens region of the state. The local magazine is titled "Pine Straw," which gives the news of the week of the pine tree happenings.

Maybe someone can explain how a neighboring town has the out-of-character name of "Aberdeen?"

The bottom level of the MC, an underbelly of the elegant and chandeliered grand foyer, was home to the members' locker room—the pro's hangout prior to their practices and the day's pairings. The massive main foyer served as a volunteer rendezvous point for the fifteen volunteers working their four-hour shifts inside and outside the MC. The clients of the corporate businesses represented in the main ballrooms upstairs had to show their credentials, with "MC" clearly stamped on the reverse of the dangling tags they wore. They typically attached them to their belt loops or wore them around their neck like a coach's whistle. We were to check the credentials of corporate members and guests before allowing entrance to prevent any scallywags from pursuing their dreams of free food, beer, and mixed drinks offered by the corporate bigs. From the foyer, two circular stairways poured into the four main ballrooms, a utopia for business networkers.

The volunteers worked diligently to ensure the privacy of the corporate parties being held inside. Most of the guests were friendly, courteous, and appreciative of the attentiveness of the volunteers. A few guests managed their way through sixteen security checkpoints and wandered onto the second level balcony, only to be turned away for not being "credentialed enough." One such guest turned out to be the one and only President and CEO of BlueCross BlueShield Insurers of North Carolina. With clenched teeth and squinting eyes, she glared at me as I turned her away from her own party. Like an angry bull charging down the streets of Pamplona, her eyes seemed to want to gore my very existence and to trample and toss me aside like a ragdoll.

"I don't need any identification," she gruffly informed me. "I have been here all week long."

"Ma'am, you still need to have the MC badge and this wrist band," I retorted, referring to the paper bands we attached to all of the members' wrists, much like the express line identification bands at Disney World.

"You don't know me—I am the CEO of BlueCross BlueShield."

"And you don't know me—I am guardian of the great indoors beyond," I snorted. "Until I see some identification, you are not entering. Our directions were explicit—not to allow anyone inside unless they have the MC tag of the day. Today the color is brown."

As we battled for the handle of the glass doorway, the roving volunteer shift supervisor overheard the ruckus and entered the fray. Glenda Takagishi, a quiet, kind, and gentle lady was in her fifth consecutive year as volunteer for the U.S. Open. Her status as a seasoned veteran enabled her to calmly and succinctly handle the dispute. Alas, the confronting woman was the CEO.

"But can you at least lower the premium payments for BlueCross BlueShield participants??" I snuck in the last verbal punch.

Ms. Takagishi, I learned, was from faraway San Francisco. I also learned that she could not speak a word of Japanese, although her name suggested otherwise. Reminiscent of Mr. Miagi from *Karate Kid,* she was soft-spoken yet firm. Later that day, a young Japanese man with a "Player Assistant" nametag approached, along with his young wife and teenage daughter.

"Excuse, pweez, I am wooking for 'lules office pwace,'" he said in super-slow motion replay video mode.

"What are you looking for?" the two of us echoed at the same time.

"The 'lules committee pwace.'" Again, ever so slowly.

"Hmmm… haven't heard of that. This is Member's Clubhouse."

"We were sent here, from USGA official. Wan to make legister for Women's Golf."

After receiving more blank looks from us, the man asked Ms. Takagishi, "Do you speak Japanese?"

Very good assumption, I thought. "No sorry, I do not," she replied.

Through some awkward reasoning and a lengthy discussion, we finally realized that he had been directed to the Rules Committee, which had set up the registration entry for the Women's' Open tryouts and qualifying. Their makeshift office trailer was located behind the clubhouse, a mere two hundred yards away. The trio was then escorted to the trailer, where the young teenage phenome would be able to register for the U.S. Women's' Open, being held for the first time in history the following week at the same course.

To all golf fans, I recommend working as a volunteer at a professional tournament near your home. You'll have unique experiences and make memories that will last a lifetime, thanks to the "characters" just waiting to be discovered. I expect to meet many more in future tournaments as both a volunteer and a spectator.

CHAPTER 3

Cousin Charlie's Fault

It was all my cousin Charlie's fault. Technically speaking he was my cousin-in-law, since he was married to my dad's sister's daughter. He and Mary were also my godparents. As godparents, they had looked out for my overall health and wellbeing since birth. Cousin and Godfather Charlie kept an interest in my upbringing, especially when it came to my developments in sports.

We called him "Chaa-lee," with a discernable New Yorker accent, as in "Hey Chaa-lee, how ya doin'?" For us it was always "Mary and Chaa-lee." It was rare to use only Chaa-lee's name without mentioning Mary, his wife. We would say things like, "You know Mary and Chaa-lee? Well, Chaa-lee is coming over later today and then he's going to get new tires on his car." Chaa-lee always made a big deal out of getting new tires for his car. Because we lived in New York State, the threat of a big snow was always a possibility in the winter. Chaa-lee had an annual ritual of replacing his regular summer tires with special winter snow tires, usually the kind with metal studs on the tread. In March of each year his tire-changing ritual was reversed when he replaced the snow tires with the normal "summer wear" tires, once the threat of snowy weather had passed.

This was big news for Mary and Chaa-lee. He'd announce it to all of us the week he'd undergo this significant event. He was never sure if a 4-ply tire was any better than the conventional 2-ply tire, and this became a source of intense debate between Chaa-lee and my dad as I listened in. Back in the Fifties and Sixties, radial tires did not exist, and the 4-ply tire was a new commodity on the tire market; it wasn't readily accepted by most people because it didn't yet have a strong reputation. The older-style tires, the type with the rubber inner tube, had to be chosen from two types. The 4-ply looked exactly like the 2-ply, yet they had an extra layer of rubber membrane on the inside lining. But many car owners were hesitant to pay the extra five bucks. I guess the tire makers either couldn't count very well, or more likely didn't believe that drivers would think that just one more ply would be enough to get them to buy a mere 3-ply tire, so they skipped right to the 4-ply. But since both types of tire did not last very long, maybe twenty thousand to twenty-five thousand miles each, this tire-changing ritual became as frequent as the practice of rotating tires every several thousand miles for the best and longest tread life. Chaa-lee had to have the best tires for his '57 Chevy Bel Air four-door sedan because "You gotta have good tires—what good is a car without good tires?"

After much discussion, cousin Chaa-lee would leave it up to the local tire expert to decide the better of the two types of tires. "I'm going to Cooley's—he has every type of tire you would want." Cooley or Mr. Cooley, I'm not sure if that was his first name, last name or nickname, owned a small garage filled with tires. That was all, just tires. He was the local tire expert specializing in 2-ply, 4-ply, and snow tires, and in all the sizes needed for cars back then, which weren't many at all. White wall tires had to be special ordered at least three weeks before they were needed. It was not your conventional garage nor was Cooley your typical garage mechanic. He wore a long-sleeved white shirt with a thin black necktie, and black chinos with a pressed sheen. He chomped on a six-inch chubby cigar from which he blew locomotive smoke rings. His place was unadvertised and unknown except to the locals who needed tires changed or rotated. His garage was located down a long alleyway off a neighborhood street and he worked out of a totally unmarked building. Maybe Chaa-lee was patronizing a black market tire dealer or maybe a mafia cover-up disguised as a business. Was this guy's real name Cooliano? Come to think of it, Chaa-lee seemed to visit far too many times for just regular tire needs, and when he mentioned the name "Cooley," he usually did so in a low, whispering voice as he scanned over the immediate horizon for any potential listeners.

Our family never owned or used specially-made snow tires for the winter months. "Too darned expensive," Dad said, and besides, "Where are you going to put them in the spring, summer, and fall of the year?" Dad never said "autumn." He only referred to autumn as the "fall of the year." "People don't know how to drive in the snow, especially young people. They got no business driving in this weather," he'd complain.

Unfortunately for Chaa-lee and many others, it was necessary to drive to work in those conditions whether they wanted to or not. Dad and the rest of our family didn't work in the winter because he owned a family ice cream business, which he closed from November through February of each year. So, we actually didn't have any business driving in the snow. We did, however, install a set of tire chains on the rear tires of the family Ford station wagon, the real classy type with the faux wood paneling on the side, prior to all significant snowfall events. One, two, or three inches of snowfall was not a significant enough event for installing a set of tire chains. Dad's personal definition of significant snow accumulation was at least six inches or more. That amount of snow would hang around the streets for quite a while during those cold, wintry days in New York State. The ultimate decision to install the snow tires came by way of sticking a yardstick in the snow in two different places. The first reading was taken in the backyard, outside the back door of the house. If that passed the six-inch test, then the second yardstick reading was taken on the driveway of our house. "Nobody drives on lawns, so it has to be taken on pavement, where you drive," Dad would say. Made a lot of sense to us.

Dad wasn't a weatherman, but he seemed to know more about upcoming weather in our town than did the weatherman on TV or radio. Snow coming from the south was always more dangerous than snow from the west or northwesterly direction. It was usually heavier, wetter, and resulted in more accumulation than the other types of snow. With a large accumulation of snow covering everything, Dad, Chaa-lee, and his buddies discussed the difficulty of clearing the roadways and would rhetorically exclaim, "Where ya' gonna' put it all?" Fortunately, the low-lying hilltops surrounding the town served as a funnel to ward off and deflect some of the worst effects of snow or thunderstorms in the summer. Weathermen weren't aware of these phenomena, but locals were keen to them.

With a labor force of five young boys not yet in college, Dad was able to install and remove tire chains all winter long. Under his supervision we placed them on the tires with exactly the right method, which often involved rocking the car forward or backwards to get the chains on tight. "Make sure they're good 'n tight, I don't want any chains clanging on the roads or falling off." Placing chains on the tires was hard work, especially in the colder weather with our bare hands. Gloves prevented us from getting the proper grip on the chains.

Because the chains were sold as one-size-fits-all types, it was often the case that the actual chain was longer than required for the circumference of the tire. Tightfitting each chain was a chore. The greater number of links left over after spreading the chain across the tire meant the tighter the chain was. Dad would then put a dab of paint on one of the links, which allowed us to check that the chain stayed at a minimally acceptable level of tightness and was therefore road-worthy. All of this was accomplished with snow on the ground, in freezing 20-degree temperatures and howling winds, with gloveless hands and frostbitten fingers—though at least we were warmed by the ten layers of bulky clothing that took over thirty minutes to put on before heading out.

Because the dab of paint Dad placed on certain links would wear off at the end of the winter, we'd all guess during the first snowfall of the year which link it would be. This debate would last longer than the time it took to actually put the chains on. Once we had tightened the chains, Dad would pop up and declare, "Nope, two more links oughta do it," then retreat for a short time—about the time it would take to drink a steaming hot cup of coffee to warm up from the frozen tundra, grab the paint, and color-code the winning links. On the outside of each tire and tire chains we'd place a four-pronged spring tensioner, which when affixed to the chain helped to tighten and keep it in place. This was like adding a toy slinky spider web to the mix. It usually resulted in pinched fingers unless you popped your eye out first when the spring struck back. You bet we were all happy after the final snowfall of the season when Dad declared, "Hang the chains on the nails in the garage for next year." Spring was a welcome time of the year, since we didn't have to store four bulky snow tires for the spring, summer, and "fall of the year."

Cousin Chaa-lee was about twenty years older than me—everyone in my parents' family had married later in their lives, resulting in many of my cousins being somewhat older than me. He worked hard at his job in the gypsum plant over in Peekskill, about twenty miles away. He worked his way up to foreman and made a decent living for Mary and himself in a middle-class neighborhood. They didn't have children of their own, so my brothers and sisters and I were somewhat of a surrogate family to him. His annual two-week vacation came in the summer, yet he never really took a long vacation away from home. The majority of his vacation was spent painting the garage, cleaning out the attic, refurbishing the window screens, replacing linoleum in the kitchen, fixing up the push mower, and other summertime projects that you just can't escape if you own a house. One summer he and Mary visited the Jersey Shore for a two-night stay. Not one to brag, he relayed those memories to us many times in the coming years, proud to enjoy a few days away from home.

He came to watch many of our little league baseball games held in the summer evenings, as baseball consumed much of our family's life. My four brothers and I started out in the t-ball league, and with an overwhelming amount of backyard practice, made it up to the "major league" of our Little League organization. The town had "minor league" teams, too, for the kids who wanted to play but were still one step away from "the Bigs." Little League baseball was an important event in town, with only thirty-five miles separating us from downtown New York City and the likes of the Bronx Bombers Yogi Berra, Whitey Ford, Roger Maris, and "the Mick" Mickey Mantle, among other New York Yankees. But I was a National League fan (of the New York Giants in particular), and because our major league consisted of only National League teams, I played on the Giants. Besides, the minor league teams were all named after American League teams. One of my older brothers played on the White Sox before he was "called up" to the big time.

Our 1957 All-Star team made it all the way to the New York State championship game and won the Little League state title that year. We had other successful years subsequent to that year, often going to the state semis or finals before being knocked out of the single round elimination games. Much of this success was due to our perennial All-Star Coach, Jim "the Iceman" Nixon, a dedicated baseball guy in town. He was the Iceman not because he was cold and cruel to the kids on his teams, but just the opposite, at least in my case. He worked at the Ice House, a business that provided crushed and cubed ice and delivered it to homes and businesses. It's true that in the summer days leading up to all-star games, he'd hold two-a-day practices for his teams, which lasted two hours each morning and three hours each night under the "major league lights." The teams practiced hard under the no-nonsense Coach Iceman Nixon. These days, kids complain, parents sue, and every move of the coach is scrutinized. But back in the glory days, the kids felt honored to be chosen for the all-star team and just wanted to play ball the right way under a knowledgeable coach. We had that in the Iceman.

Our success was also a result of the tremendous support and efforts of the parents and others in town, like my cousin Chaa-Lee. He came to our games, hung out and draped himself over the right field fence line, near the foul pole with his buddies "Old Man McCormick," "Chubby Cornwell," "Mick O'Rourke," and usually my dad, too. I can still hear Chaa-Lee shouting to us, "Show 'em how to eat soup with a shovel." Never quite knew what that was all about, but at least I knew he was rooting for our side, and never heard anyone else use that phrase.

Cousin Chaa-lee talked sports and played the occasional round of golf during his "vacation weeks," that is, after he cleaned the gutters, washed and waxed the car, got the tires rotated at Cooley's, drove Mary to the hairdresser, took a drive to the Paramus, New Jersey mall—the closest establishment to real urban-type shopping—and helped his in-laws with their household heavy work. It didn't leave much time for golf, but as he was cleaning out his garage one summer, he realized he had not one but two sets of clubs. The second set was tucked way in the corner, hidden behind stacks of dilapidated boxes filled with old paint cans, paint brushes, old clothing-turned-rags used for painting projects or changing oil in his car, an extra rusted lawnmower blade because "You never know when it will come in handy," and other forgotten items. The golf bag was a lightweight carry bag with a few odd clubs that he remembered purchasing at a yard sale many years earlier. He planned to use this set in the future rather than having to lug a full set up and down the hills. Chaa-lee knew that I liked different sports, and after years of little league baseball and now playing high school baseball, he invited me to join him in an afternoon of golf. It was then that I was formally introduced to the game.

The invitation to play came out of nowhere. Chaa-lee felt the need to get out of the house for the afternoon and informed Mary he was going over to Pearl River to check on a few important things needed for the house. Technically, this was an honest excuse, and any judge in a court of law would agree with this, since we did stop at a Dutch Boy paint shop to look at paint colors along the route to the Blue Hills Golf Course in Pearl River. Being ever so cautious, he backed his BelAir close up to his detached garage so as not to be seen stashing two sets of clubs in his trunk—otherwise his neighbors would've been suspicious.

Any previous golfing experience for me had come in the way of a practice range near the drive-in movie theater several miles from home. It was a combination outdoor theater, miniature golf course and driving range off a secondary road. A teenage hangout. Clubs could be rented there, so I figured it would be a great place to take my seventeen-year-old date. We could try to hit some golf balls, play some putt-putt, and share some popcorn and Pepsi all in one Saturday evening.

What girl wouldn't love such a romantic time? Hey, at least we'd be under the summer night stars. True, they'd be somewhat blotted out by the bright overhead lights surrounding the driving range, but there were stars up there.

My set from Chaa-lee was labeled "Walter Hagen Classics," the name stamped on each odd numbered iron. The steel of the shafts was slightly rusted and they had real blades, the only kind available then. The cavity-backed ones didn't appear until many years later, in the late Eighties, I believe. The driver was a small persimmon-woodened heavy-duty club, most likely used as a weapon in the First World War. It was slightly bent from its years of storage in the garage against a box of some old paint cans, but usable for a first time hacker. There was also a persimmon head 3-wood in decent shape but, upon eyeing it for the first time, I wasn't sure when a 3-wood could be used out there. Apparently the original owner of the clubs wasn't sure when to use the 3-wood either, as it was the best-looking club in the bag. Honestly, I didn't know which clubs were best to use at any time, with the exception of the driver and putter. Not that it mattered much; all my shots ended up at nearly the same distance anyway, so I stuck to the driver, 5-iron, and putter for most of my initial round with my cousin.

The 7 clubs came with a yellowed canvas carry bag, which was at one time paper-white, but left to the natural elements had turned dingy. The strap was brittle, cracked, dried out leather, with texture of a hardened and wrinkled catcher's mitt left out in the rain then dried. Not exactly "Fine Corinthian Leather," it was torn in a few places but it did the job. Chaa-lee offered to buy some new balls at the club pro shop, but when we discovered quite a few old brownish-colored Spaulding balls in the pockets, we decided against anything newer. Besides, he had paid the ten bucks for me to golf. "Let's not get extravagant right away," he said, "I ain't J. Rockafeller, you know."

His clubs and bag were newer, produced sometime in the early twentieth century, nicely shined and barely used. The bag was made of heavy-looking brown leather, a look that complemented Chaa-lee's industrious down-to-earth personality. Hell, no, we weren't riding in a cart or pulling our bags with a walk-behind pull cart, not even a thought was given to that. "Golf is a sport to be walked and enjoyed for the exercise," he proclaimed. So he taught me my first lesson: how to sling the bag over my shoulder and carry it.

I teed up my golf ball on the first hole and as I practiced swinging wildly like a madman trying to smack a deceitful swarming fly in the living room with a fly swatter, Chaa-lee gave me a few tips on producing a slower swing and making contact with the ball. "It's easier than hitting an eighty-mile-an-hour fastball, 'cause the ball ain't moving," he reassured me. "Try to stay calm, think of something relaxing and fun to do, and take a deep breath before smacking the ball." All I could think of right then was the time on the driving range when I tried to impress my girlfriend. She smiled sweetly and then laughed hysterically when the ball dribbled quietly off the driving range mat. That thought-provoking tactic didn't work, but thanks anyway, Chaa-lee. I gritted my teeth even tighter, now even tenser than before his attempted mental conditioning.

It was past my time to tee off, and I was already "on the clock" according to the friendly, yet stodgy, white-haired old starter. "Is it safe to hit?" I questioned, eyeing the group in the carts ahead, just over the crest of the fairway and nearly out of sight. I had no sense of distance as to how far my ball could potentially travel. Many years later, the Army would teach me to evaluate distances in a truck convoy by counting the telephone poles on the sides of the road. The distance between each pole is roughly one hundred yards, and truck drivers are trained to remain at least one pole behind the truck in front of them in order to keep a safe and constant distance apart. With ten trucks in a convoy, there should be a distance of ten poles from the first truck to the last. Even on the golf course today, I still sometimes visualize those telephone poles to estimate my shot distances. No need for those GPS instruments or yard books used in today's modern game, no sir. Just remember the telephone poles.

Unfortunately during my initial round there were no GPS systems, and the Army was still in my future. No way to use my valuable military training here. In addition, there weren't any telephone poles on the golf course or paved cart paths to use as road markers, only a wide-open field of fairway.

"No problem at all," both the grumpy starter with gunfighter stare and Chaa-lee announced at the same time and in the same accusatory tone of voice, urging me to start the first-ever round of my career.

"Please don't strike out," I reminded myself as I instantly thought about "Casey at the Bat" in Mudville that day. Taking a hard, baseball-like swing, choking the club handle with a baseball grip, I made contact with the ball, which lurched forward in a fairly straight line and sailed farther than any of us on the teeing area thought it would. The old man starter and Charlie watched with me as the ball climbed over the crested fairway near the tops of the two carts and their occupants parked on the opposite downslope. Yikes! They didn't move when they should have. Nobody thought this scrawny seventeen-year-old kid with a baseball mentality could have whacked the ball out near those carts. Chaa-lee certainly didn't, although he followed with a beautiful drive of his own down the middle and up to the top of the hill.

We walked quickly to our balls, and after reaching the first green with many more chunky shots, Chaa-lee hustled over to the people in the cart and apologized for the newbie hitting his first drive over their heads. "No problem at all—we totally understand," they said politely with automatic golf etiquette, though I noticed a slight sneer that seemed to indicate, "Don't do that again, you punk."

Whew—we were both relieved to hear that. With that one tremendous drive, I was hooked on this game. Forever.

The following year, my senior year in high school, three friends and I came up with a brilliant scheme to skip a day of school. Knowing that graduation was right around the corner and that we were all in good standing, we figured we'd be able to get away with it. But our planning had to be flawless in order to defeat the notorious school-wide and countywide truancy officer, Mr. Farr. Not only did Mr. Farr know all the kids in the high school and kept a running total of their absences throughout the school year, but he also knew every parent, grandparent, and local relative of the kids in our school. As he roamed the hallways each morning before the school bell rang, he would check for violations of dress code and other instances of rule breaking. He observed the kids' behavior and noise level while walking the hallways and had absolutely no tolerance for running inside the school, as well as for loitering in front of lockers. He alone determined both the appropriate and inappropriate behaviors of us high school students.

Upon seeing Mr. Farr for the very first time each morning, we were expected to greet him with a sincere, "Good morning, Mr. Farr. How are you?" After being a truancy officer for thirty years at the same school and living in the same town and in the same house for all that time, his ability to figure out who were the troublemakers on any particular day was unparalleled. Looking down at the floor or up at the ceiling when passing Mr. Farr seemed to him to be an indicator of avoidance and of potential trouble. It was "student profiling" at its finest.

Mr. Farr had his own small truancy office near the front door of our high school, and when late students came through the hallways without a parent's signed excused note, he would herd them to his small office for questioning. Before releasing them to their first period homeroom class, he made a phone call to the parents of the perp. The outside of his office was reminiscent of the 'Go to Jail' corner of the Monopoly board game. Metal bars lined the outside of a sliding wooden window where students could talk to him as if they were talking to a bank teller during the Wild West days. Basically, his office had been designed the way bank interiors were designed to thwart potential bank robbers.

After taking daily attendance, our homeroom teachers dutifully sent the attendance roster down to Mr. Farr by way of a reliable student messenger. Absentees were highlighted, and upon receiving this roster Mr. Farr made a personal phone call to every one of the parents of the students in question. His procedure appeared absolutely impenetrable to teenagers trying to crack the system. But we had to try. As Yoda famously said in one of the *Star Wars* movies, "There is do or don't do; there is no try." Surely, four college-bound students could outwit one crusty old truancy officer. After all, the four of us had all passed Mrs. Riley's 301 and 302 Biology classes, not to mention Ms. Davies' Advanced Latin classes, both major hurdles for future college entrants.

We had agreed upon the plan the previous day. We would all arrive at school on time as on any other normal spring day, greet Mr. Farr in the usual manner and scurry on to our home-room first period so that we would be listed as present for the day. The second classroom period was our P.E. hour, where-upon we'd change into our red P.E. shorts and t-shirts embla-zoned with the high school logo and adorned with red-trim sleeves and neckline. During warmer weather, the class of roughly thirty students would be outdoors learning and play-ing a vague form of soccer, taught to us by the coach and P.E. teacher, Mr. Sterling. Mr. Sterling doubled as the boys head basketball coach during the basketball season, and the boys J.V. baseball coach in the spring. He knew all four of us quite well since we had played J.V. baseball the previous years and had tried out unsuccessfully for the varsity basketball team our senior year. He certainly would vouch for our attendance at P.E. that day.

I was cut from the varsity basketball team on the fourth and last day of tryouts mostly due to my poor shooting, though also for attempting a twenty-foot hook shot from near the top of the key, much like Kareem Abdul Jabar of the Los Angeles

Lakers executing his infamous sky hook. Dougie Margiotta was cut from the basketball team on day two of tryouts simply because this "burly forward" tried to muscle his way through the defender while making layups. At five foot ten, Dougie was a top-rated 180-pound heavy weight wrestler on the wrestling team, which did not help him at all on the basketball court. Gary McKenna was a fine athlete who often hosted pick-up basketball games in his parent's backyard driveway. He played four years of high school baseball alongside me, and was also cut from tryouts on day two because he didn't believe in or practice any defense, which was a trademark of Coach Sterling's. Jim Scott or "Scottso," the same Scottso who traveled around Florida with me to watch Major League Baseball spring training and the Honda Classic Golf Tournament forty-six years later, was also cut from basketball. He was too short, too uncoordinated for basketball, and way too hotheaded for the likes of the coach. Scottso was the original Tasmanian Devil cartoon character when it came to sports, and especially when it came to losing. His physique was better suited for wrestling, which he excelled in the middleweight class. Four years of high school grappling resulted in his pug-like nose and crooked smile from hours on the mats. Sometime during those years he broke his left pinkie finger, which never set correctly allowing normal straightening and remains as an archway with the knuckle protruding skyward. His golf grip was affected since he couldn't place pressure on the club with the lower most tips of his fingers. It didn't alter his game at all since he swung the club as though he was smashing at a piñata lowered to the ground.

We soon forgave Coach Sterling for his misgivings and his desire to rebuild the team with a youth movement made up of mostly sophomores and juniors. Except that the team could have used a six-foot-one senior rebounder with a surprising hook shot to confuse the opposition, instead of the chosen six-foot-three sophomore string bean center, all of 150 pounds with spindly arms and thin-as-spaghetti-noodle legs. And no doubt Dougie could have been the enforcer beneath the boards, not on account of his great leaping ability, but through his unmatched strength in bludgeoning his opponents.

After the P.E. hour of outdoor soccer, we headed back to the locker room and changed back into our school/golf clothes for the day. We had devised a perfect escape plan on a perfectly warm day, and looked forward to a perfect day ahead. We slipped out the back door of the school, which was fortunately located near the school gym and its accompanying locker rooms. Undetected and with swift, stealthy movements that any Navy Seal Team would've envied, we hopped into Gary McKenna's dad's 1950 Ford Galaxy, cleverly pre-positioned on the adjoining neighborhood street at the rear of the school and gym access rear door. A perfect getaway.

The getaway car, the 1950 Ford Galaxy 500, was a monstrous black beauty. It had a manual transmission with the shift lever on the steering column, a heavy clutch, an AM radio allowing us to listen to WABC's Cousin Brucey play the sounds of the late Sixties all day, bench seats both front and back, and enough interior space to fit an entire VW Beetle bug. To us it was a luxury limo even without any air conditioning, though we did have the 4-55 that we used in the summer months— four windows rolled down while going 55 miles per hour. Two of us sitting in the comfortable back seat, scrunched down like gangsta hit men on a takedown mission, ready to spring into action, we felt perfectly content.

The car quietly rolled out of town, Gary carefully avoiding Main Street and other main arteries leading downtown where the school was located. Once free from town central, we traveled forty-five minutes over back roads leading to the Blue Hills Golf Course in Pearl River. Yes, the very same course that cousin Chaa-lee and I had escaped to ten months earlier, where I suspected that many other community weekend golfers would rendezvous to in order to avoid chores on sunshine-filled weekends. Our escape was made on a Friday, and the plan was working.

Every golfer playing the Blue Hills Course had to sign in before play, which I learned while playing with Chaa-lee. With this knowledge, we gladly assumed the role of the teenage wise guys out to outsmart the old-timers. On paper, we became Pete Nicklaus, Dougie Palmer, Gary Player, and Jim Trevino. The pro shop manager didn't look at the names right away as we checked in but probably had good suspicion that we were not really Nicklaus, Palmer, Player, and Trevino. The old man starter gave a quiet laugh and chuckle as he announced, "Mr. Nicklaus, your foursome is next on the tee."

What a glorious day it was; no school classrooms, no teachers, no Mr. Farr, plenty of brilliant sunshine, puffy clouds like oversized golf balls, Shamrock-green fairways with tall pines, cedars, and oak trees bordering the outside edges of the rough. We walked with our bags slung over our shoulders, mine on loan from Chaa-lee since we last played; Dougie, Gary, and Scottso's slipped from their dad's garages in the hopes of not being discovered missing that day.

Our day finished right around the time the last school bell would ring, marking the end of the academic day—perfect timing to return back home without suspicion from parents or others who cared. We melted back into Gary's dad's black car that had been sitting in the hot sun for over four hours, feeling somewhat refreshed once the windows were down and the car was in motion. We were on the road to happiness, listening once again to Cousin Brucey and singing along to the radio tunes of the Rolling Stones. "I can't get no satisfaction, but I tried and I tried, but I can't get me no-satisfaction." "Hey, hey, hey." Those Sixties songs had a lot of "Hey, hey, hey" or "Baby, baby, baby" in them, easy to sing along to even if you didn't know the lyrics, which we usually didn't, although we pretended we did.

My personal favorite was "Mustang Sally" by Wilson Pickett. It had a great beat and was meaningful to us at the time. "He brought her a brand new Mustang, a 1965, Mustang Sally, you'd better slow your Mustang down." "Oh, Lord." My grandfather had a Ford dealership in town, so quite naturally our family owned Ford cars. When Mustangs became a popular muscle car, this song made the car even more popular. Dougie's parents had given him a nearly new 1964 Mustang convertible, bright pumpkin orange with a black ragtop, purchased from my grandfather's business. They planned this in advance of his upcoming graduation. He was the oldest of six children and his parents wanted to impress upon the others how important a diploma could be, laying the groundwork for college and work beyond. As the song came on the radio, we replaced "Sally" with "Dougie" as we accompanied Wilson Pickett. "Mustang Dougie…"

Gary took the same secondary country road that we came in on. On both sides of the road were wide-open fields of tall grass and not much else. It was as if the slightest breeze made the grasses sway and wave to us as we drove past, as if they were saying, "Have a nice day." The middle of the afternoon was upon us, and there wasn't a car in sight on this lonely, curvy two-lane back road. Listening and occasionally singing along to the radio, chatting about our daylong adventure while the hospitable summer-like breezes cooled us off made the trip worthy of a scene from *Bueller's Day Off.*

Suddenly a car approached us from the opposite direction, the first we had seen since leaving the Blue Hills parking lot. "Hey, doesn't your dad own a car like that?" inquired Scottso, now commandeering the front passenger seat.

"Yes, something like that," Gary answered, "but that can't be him 'cause he's at work."

As the car slipped past us in the opposite lane, Scottso alertly perked up. "Gary, that looked like your dad driving that car."

"You know something, guys, that was my dad, but I don't think he saw us. He was going too fast," Gary reassured us.

"Do you think he recognized this car?" two of us immediately and nervously questioned from the back seat.

"Don't know."

"He must've seen us—there are probably only one or two big black Fords like this one in the whole county."

"Hell, John Glenn would be able to spot this black marble from his Mercury Space Capsule orbiting the earth twenty-five miles up. He had to have noticed it."

It didn't help much when the car allegedly containing Gary's dad suddenly slowed down for no apparent reason. We all turned to watch his brake lights beam their bright red flash of doom in our direction.

"Let's hurry up and get back to your house ahead of him, so he can't claim he saw us." A brilliant plan on Scottso's part and the same conclusion we all simultaneously concluded.

Before heading home, Gary dropped me off at my house. As the enormous and bulky black beauty rumbled its way to the top of the hill and driveway surrounding our house, I was instantly relieved to discover that our family's Ford station wagon was not in sight. Whew—that meant Mom was out doing her daily shopping and afternoon errands. Dad was at work, at the family business. I quietly and stealthily put the borrowed clubs back in their rightful place in the detached, barn-style garage. We kept everything from lawn mowers and rusty infrequently-used tools, to baseball bats, paint cans, snow shovels, and those winter tire chains stored in this garage. There was even a very old wooden canoe with a large hole in its side about the size of a fist stored in the rickety rafters alongside two unpainted paddles. Lots of things were kept in this Forties built garage, everything but a car.

It was a perfect reentry after the day's events. Mom arrived an hour later and asked why I wasn't at baseball practice.

"Coach Filor cancelled it, he had something important to do— an appointment with his dentist," I responded. It was true.

"Oh, how did you do on Mr. Mello's history quiz?"

"I'm not sure, they weren't graded in class." It wasn't true.

The four of us shared third period in Mr. Mello's World History class. I anxiously remembered that Mr. Anthony Mello was a friend of my parents as he had previously taught three of my older siblings. He routinely assessed my grasp of history by comparing my performance to that of my siblings. As per usual, I came in fourth.

Mom merely shrugged her shoulders, looked me straight in the eyes and remarked, "I'm sure you did okay, your grades are very good. Besides, it was a perfect day for school and other things."

I think she knew, she had to have known, but for some reason she didn't let on. It was the way she said "and other things." She was nodding her head up and down while smiling these words. Many years later, I still wonder if she knew about our trip.

Gary got home in time, ahead of his mean-as-a-pit-bull father. But from that day forward we never got to ride in that car again, and for the rest of our high school days and the summer after, I never saw Gary drive it.

Golf is a sport that binds friendships together whether starting at an early age or later in life. The memory of escaping out the back door of our high school and enjoying that April school day basking in the sunshine of freedom is a highlight of teenage years. All of this started with thanks in large part to Cousin Charlie.

CHAPTER 4

Patrick, Patrick, and Patrick

MEETING THREE PEOPLE in the same week with the same first name, and all who love to play golf together, is unusual. I think the chances of that happening are astronomical. Maybe not quite astronomical, but the odds are very high indeed. According to a friend of mine who just loves statistical analysis and putting everything into numerical categories, Judy McElroy has figured that the odds of that happening are about one in 350. So I guess this type of thing occurs more often than I thought. However, in all my years I can't think of more than five guys named Patrick, and three of them I met at the same time within seven days of each other. Now what you think about that, Statistician McElroy?

I nicknamed my best golfing buddy over the past eight years "Air Force Patrick" in order to differentiate one Patrick from two others. Air Force Patrick spent twenty-two years in the Air National Guard and retired with the noncommissioned rank of Technical Sergeant, E6. Most of his twenty-two years were spent sitting behind a supply desk or shuffling papers in the personnel office. Whenever we meet new players on the first tee, Air Force Patrick enjoys recounting his military experience to the newcomers. After hearing the stories over and over and over, I remind him that his job title and duties are referred to as "Chair-borne" in the Army. Many Army soldiers are Airborne-qualified or Air Assault-qualified and, in either case, must undergo rigorous training and conduct multiple parachute jumps or helicopter rope rappelling exercises. Becoming Airborne is a highly demanding process, and receiving Airborne wings is a highly cherished honor. Same is true for receiving the "Air Assault Badge." A pencil pushing, paper moving, administrative personnel specialist requires little physical training but must be able to endure many hours sitting behind a desk in a comfortable chair. And minimal physical training suits Patrick's five-foot-eight pot-bellied physique. Now entering his sixth decade on planet Earth, his overall appearance belies his chronological age. He seems to be many years younger still retaining mostly darkened, straight flat, fluffy hairstyle. All natural. He runs his fingers through his locks as if a movie star and believes he could have made it alongside Clint Eastwood or Paul Newman as a young man.

To his credit, Air Force Patrick received his college degree and learned valuable and much-needed skills with the Air Force as a contract specialist. In civilian life he continues to work for the Department of Defense using his skills as a senior contract specialist and now teaches younger Airmen and Technical Sergeants the finer points about completing contracts with the Air Force and Army.

I gave the second Patrick the title of "Army Patrick," a sensible name given that he was an active duty officer with over fourteen years of Army experience. A married man with two small children, his free time to play golf is somewhat limited, even though living on an Army post just a few minutes from the golf course has afforded him time to practice his game. Most of his friends and acquaintances refer to him as Pat, a very non-descriptive name. So he was understandably very honored by his new moniker, Army Patrick. He is one hundred percent Army, immersed in the Army way of life. He was deployed to two combat zones in a matter of three years and was promoted to Lieutenant Colonel for his efforts, dedication, and leadership.

There is something strange about Army Patrick, a true Army logistician, who can strategically work his way out of any difficult task or assignment that confronts him. He is the officer's version of Corporal Klinger from *MASH*. He is a unique combination of serious and laid-back, nonchalant about most things. This includes his golf game where he doesn't get very concerned about his score. He merely wants to hit decent, respectable shots. His beer of choice (and only choice) is Heineken when on the course. Oh, and not in cans, either— only from those dark green bottles with the "real" caps, the kind that don't twist off. Great, it isn't easy to find a bottle opener out on the far reaches of the open course. Although it's a delicious and refreshing beer when served cold, it's not worth the frustrating hassle to open the darn thing when you just want to satisfy your thirst in the hot sun. It is according to Army Patrick. He is serious about the brew, juxtaposed with his nonchalant feelings about his score.

Army Patrick didn't smoke at all when we first met him. But Air Force Patrick and I cured him of that; after only two rounds of cart golf he was enticed to join us and "smoke 'em if you got 'em.'" Army Patrick now lights up the best Montecristo or Punch stogie while sipping his Heineken. A real connoisseur.

The third Patrick is "Dizmo Patrick," or as he prefers, "The Dizmo." Dizmo is a high energy, high maintenance type of guy. He is the one member of our foursome who owns customized clubs and a personalized leather bag. The bag itself weighs about four hundred pounds. His clubs were specifically designed and tailored to his swing by Mickey Russell. Mickey, a local club maker, previously owned a small golf shop in Yorktown, Virginia, and was a favorite among the PGA professional golfers such as Freddy Couples, Mark O' Meara, and Raymond Floyd. Mickey (now deceased, sadly) held the title of #1 professional club maker for many years—from 1970 to 1999. Dizmo was a frequent customer and often upgraded his clubs at Mickey's.

Dizmo enjoys the best of everything, including colorful matching clothes from the best designers, expensive Ecco golf shoes, and high-end golf balls. He usually arrives at the course in the newest BMW series sports car 320i, declaring, "Go large or go home." Contrast that to my twenty-year-old Ford, which suits me perfectly. This is not to say that Dizmo flaunts his ego—this is who he happens to be all the time. No façade, no pretending, no backing down. He never smoked cigars until he met Air Force Patrick and me, but has since taken up the habit on the golf course. Now he brings the twelve to twenty-dollar varieties to smoke. That's twelve to twenty dollars *each* and in a beautifully designed metal travel case that he opens and displays like it's a rare jewel case at Tiffany's.

It's always life in the fast lane with Dizmo, even in the golf cart. A word of caution: Do *not* allow Dizmo to drive your cart on any course unless you are prepared for the roller coaster carnival ride of your life and are strapped in like a NASCAR driver at Daytona. There should be a "no-cart list" patterned after the FBI's "no-fly list"—Dizmo would be at the top of the list posted in every clubhouse in the U.S.

I've been thrown out of the passenger seat twice on two mostly flat courses, thanks to his sharp turns and some unforeseen bumps. Both times we entered the rough from a 90-degree turn from the paved cart path. At Williamsburg National Golf Club, he slowed the cart down just enough in order to jump out to hit the next shot. Much like coming to an intersection in your automobile on a secondary neighborhood road and rolling through the stop sign without really stopping, Dizmo kept the cart moving forward even after hopping out of it. He didn't bother to set the parking brake; he jumped out like his hair was on fire, and on a very slight slope the cart rolled on without him. The club I tossed toward the front of the cart didn't stop the rolling thunder—doubtful that it ever could— but the cart thoughtfully came to rest about fifty yards ahead of us. "It must've been the cart's fault—faulty brakes," he announced as we joined up down the fairway. Chasing after the steamrolling cart in a slow jog was never a problem for Dizmo. Slender and very physically fit in his late thirties; he exercises daily with weight training, running, and gym room equipment. At nearly six feet tall and roughly 175 pounds, with short, cropped jet-black hair, he is a poster boy for good health and fitness.

Dizmo does everything at a fast pace, even eating. At the turn from hole #9 to tee box #10, we tend to stop for a quick lunch or beverage on the run. Quicker than you can say, "I'm hungry," Dizmo consumes his fully-loaded hot dog and half his drink. Says he has a condition that includes acid reflux that the top of his esophagus doesn't close entirely, causing him to shake, quiver, and belch numerous times before settling down. During a round at Brickshire Golf Club in New Kent, Virginia, he finished his hot dog lunch as quickly as if he had been entered in the Nathan's Coney Island hot dog eating contest on the Fourth of July. His stomach growled and his body convulsed for the next two holes, followed by something akin to a volcanic eruption. Mount St. Helens was never this volatile in its glory days. We were all ready to call in an airlift Medevac helicopter, as he lay prone not wanting to move or be moved. But at last it ended, his medical condition "emergency" was over. He then became hungry all over again, but thankfully we were too far from the clubhouse restaurant and the cart girl was nowhere in sight so a repeat performance was avoided.

Air Force Patrick, Army Patrick, and Dizmo Patrick all have one other thing in common. Occasionally they become hot-tempered. Not the angry, aggressive kind of temper, but more like the funny to watch "Yosemite Sam" cartoonish kind of temper. It's like watching a steaming kettle of water as it comes to a boil then manifests a high pitched whistling alarm.

A former professional by the name of Ivan Gantz has gotta be a folk hero of the three Patricks.

Ivan Gantz tried, but had no success as a Tour player in the 1950s. He became somewhat of an underground legend because of his outrageous temper. His most bizarre act of anger was, after missing a crucial putt, to whack himself in the head with his putter.

"Actually, that happened a few times," Gantz once recalled, going on to describe one incident in particular. "I was playing on the Tour in Houston, at Memorial Park, and missed a short putt on the last green that would have given me a 68. Man, I raised that putter up and knocked myself in the head with it. I made a pretty good chunk in there, but didn't fall down, and I wasn't knocked cold, like a lot of people said. People exaggerate."

Unlike Ivan Gantz, Air Force Patrick doesn't even need to be on the green for his antics. During one round of play, in the middle of the fairway—yes, in the middle, after a decent drive—Air Force tried to coax his seven iron out of the bag strapped to the rear of our motorized cart. Not having a particularly good day on the course overall, he yanked his club at the top of the club head, but it wouldn't budge. Another tug and the club simply vibrated, and went nowhere. The day's temperature was soaring, as was my playing companion's, evidenced by the redness in his increasingly puffy and frustrated face. Add in the high humidity in coastal North Carolina's low country, with a heat index seemingly well over 250, and it was "snap, crackle, pop" time. His third aggressive, angry, quite violent manhandling of the club sent half of it outward and over the edge of the bag, while Air Force tumbled backward like a gymnast completing floor exercises with a flourish of a backwards flip on the mat. Like a majestic Roman Gladiator with sword held high, my buddy rebounded to his feet, revealing that the top half of the seven iron had been neatly and precisely sawed in half. He looked to me like the Statue of Liberty, minus the crown, brandishing the glorious raised torch of freedom. The sacrificial iron, along with a tee marker "souvenir" from The Pearl Golf Course currently sits prominently in a place of honor in his Man Cave.

Not to be outdone by Ivan Gantz, or that other professional club thrower, Tommy Bolt, Air Force Patrick appeared to be aiming for the unofficial world record distance of a golf club thrown into a marsh. Generations from now, when excavators are implementing new and useful methods for detecting ancient metals while dredging waterways, they will encounter the tossed Nike pitching wedge beneath the Elizabeth River that crosses the Cypress Creek Golf Course in Smithfield, Virginia. A hearty throw it was, following two dreadful chops and chunks involving three wayward balls that had landed in the marsh. The shot was intended as a lay-up to the lengthy par 4, with approach shot over marsh but was blocked by unusually high, grassy spikes protruding over the front of the green from the watery marsh. After six swings, three lost balls in the mucky graveyard, and one low-hovering helicopter pitching wedge that went spinning over the horizon, he still never reached the green. A plaque located on the very spot of the fifteenth hole from the middle of the fairway (yes, the middle) is inscribed, "The best distance ever of PW thrown to the River."

Tommy Bolt earned the reputation of "Terrible Tommy" for his temper tantrums on the course. After missing a short putt in the 1953 Tucson Open, the Terrible One threw his putter wildly over the heads of the terrified crowd surrounding the green. A rumbling "wooo-aah" came from the normally respectful, silent crowd. He did come back to win the tournament by one stroke, yet there were more episodes after that. Spectators gathered specifically to witness Tommy Bolt in a potential rage in future tournaments.

This is a case of role reversal whereby a golf pro was beaten by an amateur in the uncontested event of club throwing. In the middle of a particular distressing round of putting, Dizmo sailed his putter off the green into a nearby grove of trees. Like a backyard whirligig with arms maniacally rotating in the wind, he flung his putter, which landed midway up a tree in a pine thicket. Surprisingly enough, Dizmo putted better with his three iron the rest of the way in. The grove of trees was near the exit road that circled around the green leading away from the parking area of the clubhouse. Another of our playing partners, Johnnie Carter, took interest in its location. As we departed the course after the day, we noticed him in our car's rearview mirror retrieving the perfectly unscathed customized Ping from its nest of pine needles. We linked up with Johnnie two weeks later as we played a casual round. That day he had the best putting day of his life with his new-found short stick.

Over the years of playing with the Patricks, I've picked up on a certain "marsh-hatred syndrome" that they all share, and have developed a hunch that this specific affliction only affects golfers named Patrick. In fact, I'm submitting a proposal to the U. S. Government Agency in charge of studying the eccentric behaviors of amateur athletes. I'm thinking Health and Human Services or the CDC will accept my study after they complete their findings of how shrimps perform on a treadmill. I'd like to receive a government-paid grant to study such a golfing phenomena. I'd play golf for one year with guys named Patrick only to validate my theory. If required, I'd agree to play three times each week all over the country with all of the "golfer Patricks" in existence, and would gladly continue my research in Ireland, the original home of Patricks everywhere. After extensive research and submitting my written reports, I'd spend the following year studying the golfing behaviors of women named Pat, Patty, or Patricia.

Keeping in line with his marsh-hated syndrome, Army Patrick once chunked his approach shot from a six iron into a green-side bunker on hole #7 at Sleepy Hole Golf Club in Suffolk, Virginia. A nicely groomed public course, it presents a very demanding layout for amateurs and professionals alike. In the late 1980s and early 1990s, the LPGA's Crestar Classic was played there. Hole #18 in particular was deemed the toughest finishing hole on a public course in the state, and still is today.

Hole #7, a medium range par 3 of 165 yards, has an elevated green that slopes away from the front and left side as viewed by the golfer from the tee. Army Patrick's ball landed in the left rough, downhill from, and left of, the sand bunker. He clunked his second pitch shot into the sand and failed to get himself out on the third and fourth shots. Shot five was skinned and flew miles over the green, landing in another zip code. The sand wedge flew in the opposite direction, down the slope, with a "perfect 10" entry and landing in the marsh below, if it had been scored by Olympic judges. It landed directly in the middle of the marsh, handle sticking up as though giving us a thumbs up. Army Patrick couldn't bear to disrupt his set of recently purchased, still-glossy-without-scratches, Callaways. He went in after the offensive club, the club still protruding upward from the dingy green muck like a marshy brown cattail. Four of us made a human chain bound together with extended clubs, with Army Patrick as the leading link, dangling over the marsh. Still unable to reach the club, he inched further in as mud covered the top of his shoes, ankles, calves, and finally, half of his five foot ten body. The club was retrieved, but he was not. Stuck in the quicksand-like mud, he undeniably became part of the marsh. We could hear a "slurp, slurp" sucking sound to his movements as he extricated himself from the smelly surroundings. Half drenched in dark mud from the waist down, he looked like a clay molded, not quite hardened, statue straight out of Disney World's Haunted Mansion.

In this wacky world of Patricks, I actually happened upon a fourth one, Patrick O'Leary, at the Ryder Cup Lounge of the Carolina Hotel in Pinehurst, North Carolina. O'Leary, the food and beverage manager at the hotel's lounge, has been a constant fixture there for the past eleven years. Pinehurst was once host to the Ryder Cup matches, hence the lounge's homage. A name better suited might be the Ryder Cup *Room*, which gives the connotation of a homey, cozy atmosphere. It has a welcoming and warm fireplace at one end, and a friendly walk-up bar at the other. Ryder Cup history is retold on the walls, which display numerous artifacts and pictures.

At the corner of the bar, a place worthy of standing, with our elbows leaning in and holding on, Air Force Patrick and I discussed the day's events with Patrick O'Leary. O'Leary, half German and half Irish, has the cheerfulness of a leprechaun— a tall one, that is. "I could take over the world if I weren't such a drunk," he laughingly explained. He told me that he routinely meets and greets professional golfers who patronize the establishment, but was reluctant to divulge too much of their personal dirt that day. He did share one recent incident with me, however. A certain golf pro (who will remain nameless here) stumbled out after lunch and hours of drinks with friends and either forgot or refused to pay his tab. It was a dine-and-dash of the highest level. Weeks later, the lounge received a sizeable check with a note from the humbled visitor: "I had too many 'shots' at the 19th, it was my caddy's fault."

As Tom Hanks famously said in the movie *Forrest Gump,* "Life's like a box of chocolates, you never know what you're gonna get." Nothing could be more accurate after meeting the Patricks.

CHAPTER 5

That's Awesome, Baby!

JUST LIKE THE many personalities who play golf, there are words and phrases that can be part of the game, too. While there are phrases that are commonly used and downright annoying, there are also those that are universal and strike a chord.

Have you ever noticed how people tend to get stuck on one word or phrase and to use it over and over? Here's one of those words you hear everywhere and nearly constantly— "Awesome," as in, "That's awesome, baby." I attribute the popularity of this word and phrase to the famous college basketball announcer, Dick Vitale. When a player would make a particularly nice shot or move on the court, he would shout into the microphone, "That's awesome, baby. Just awesome." And that's just one of his many catch phrases. He started it several years ago and now it has caught on nationwide.

A guy makes a good golf shot that lands in the fairway. "That's awesome!" A guy drives a nice late-model new or used car, and "It's awesome!" A kid gets a grade of A or B in school.

"That's Awesome!" You find an unexpected dollar bill on the sidewalk, which is "awesome!" Grandma dies at the age of eighty-nine. "Awesome!" Everything and anything is now "Awesome!" a word that needs to be banned immediately. As of today I declare that "awesome" be removed from the vocabulary of golfers all over the country and banned from golf lexicon.

Needless to say, there's other phrases that can get stuck in your head from time to time. One such phrase comes from a TV analyst at the 2001 Players Championship tournament at Ponte Verda Beach, Florida. When Tiger Woods hit a fantastic shot from off the green that sunk for a birdie, the analyst declared, "That's better than most; that's better than most!" Now that sure has gotten into my head and won't leave. When I hit a decent shot and my partner says, "Hey, nice shot," my reply is usually, "Better than most!" This particular phrase can be used universally, even off the course. It can be used, for example, after a friend asks how you like his newer, recently purchased used car. You can honestly tell him, "It's better than most." When you drive past a nicely-sculpted landscape of a neighbor's yard and he asks what you think of it, you can solidly declare, "It's better than most."

There are endless scenarios during which this phrase might come in handy. When asked, "How do you like my new haircut?" for example. Or when asked how many miles per gallon the car gets on the highway, if you're a car salesman. Most importantly, when your wife asks if her new jeans make her butt look bigger, you can reply, "They're better than most."

Even my golfing buddy, Phil Gilmartin, has a phrase of his own. "PhilGil" is known as a fair weather golfer. In other words, if bad weather or even a slight chance of rain or cold is forecasted for our tee time, he'll back out of the golf commitment. He simply refuses to play. When playing on a golf-perfect day, if an unanticipated breeze overtakes us and the clouds block the sunshine temporarily, he suddenly turns into weatherman Al Roker, declaring, "There's a cold front coming." Just a simple change in the direction of the wind on a typical spring afternoon, and he'll start in with, "There's a cold front coming."

Speaking of annoying sayings on the golf course, most golfers don't like to hear about it when they hit a dreadful drive or fairway shot away from their intended target. The best policy there is to keep quiet and play on. Taking this a step further, Sam Snead reminded his playing companions not to talk to his golf ball when in motion, to wait until the ball stopped rolling and to then exclaim that it was a good shot. For example—not to tell the ball to "get in the hole" when putted. He had a huge dislike for people who talked to his ball, especially when it was on the putting surface.

Often when the putt is on the way, and it looks like a perfect shot, a partner will say, "It looks good, great putt," only to have the ball miss the cup or lip the side of the cup and veer away. Now that's frustrating. I'm with Sam Snead on this one; don't talk to the ball—the ball is gonna do what the ball is gonna do anyway. It certainly is not going to listen to you.

Another phrase I often use (that is used pretty much everywhere) can be delivered in a tone of disgust, bitterness, slight growling anger, or conversely, with eyebrow-raising disbelief. I use it in a lot of situations, and it is simply "There ya go." It can commonly be associated with poor customer service across this country, as in the case of a drive-thru service of a fast food restaurant. A simple food order is given to the pimple-faced teenager through the speaker—a regular hamburger, small order of fries, and a large coke. You drive around the building to the window, you pay your money, and then proceed to receive your food in the paper bag at the next window, only to discover that what's actually in the bag is a double-cheeseburger, no french fries, and a small Sprite. Well, "There ya go."

Now let's say you're at the grocery store and you arrive at the checkout counters to pay for your purchase. It's crowded enough that two long lines have formed. You choose line #1, which seems to contain fewer customers. As you approach the cashier and place your Items on the black conveyor belt separating you from the clerk, the person in front of you suddenly whips out his checkbook to make a payment. "Who writes a check anymore?" you ask yourself. Why, only the Fatso directly in front of you, that's who. Then and only then does he begin to fill it out. "By the way, does anyone know what the date is today?" he asks. It happens to be March 4, so he asks, "Would that be 3/ 4 or 4/ 3 when I write this?" and "How much does this come to, again?" he inquires to the ever-so-patient middle-aged clerk, who really doesn't care how much time this is taking since she gets paid by the hour anyway and not by the number of customers served.

"Oh, okay, here it is," the check writer announces, handing the check over to the ever-so-patient cashier.

"Oops, I'm sorry, sir, but the check did not clear," whispers the ever-so-patient, seemingly amused clerk after several minutes of watching the check-clearing machine make its determination.

With toes tapping, you breathe deeply and heave a big sigh as you look over at line #2, the one you didn't choose, and notice customers #4 and #5 passing quickly through the aisle and going on their happy way. They even appear to be skipping their way out through the automatic sliding doors, which are eagerly awaiting their arrival as if to say, "You have been a great customer today! Thanks for being so efficient in your purchase."

"Wow… I didn't expect this, it surely must be the bank's problem," Fatso says. "Now, where is my credit card," he mumbles to himself as he pads down every one of the twelve pockets that cover his jeans, shirt, and coat. "Honey, do you have the credit card?" he asks his wife. She idles next to him as she scans the racks reading the front covers of *The National Inquirer* and *Secrets of Hollywood Stars,* tabloids she does not intend to purchase.

"Huh? What? Oh, lemme look," she responds, foraging through her Volkswagen-sized faux leather purse with its large strap across the top and five buckles to unlock. "It's in here somewhere," she chuckles, "I had it yesterday when I went to Wal-Mart." The much-used credit card is finally handed over to the cashier as three more happy customers pass through the opposing line.

"Do you have any ID?" the amused clerk calmly asks the dynamic duo.

After a little more fumbling and digging down into the bottomless pit of her handbag, wifey discovers her driver's license with bits of chewed gum stuck to the plastic picture and carefully removes the gooey substance using her thumbnail.

"I'm glad you found yours, honey, because mine expired in February, and I guess it's time to get an updated one," informs hubby.

With the transaction now complete (in about the time it takes to watch a full nine-inning professional baseball game on TV, all six hundred commercials included) it is decision time. "Will that be plastic or paper?" the cashier inquires.

As you have already witnessed eighteen customers pass expeditiously through line #2, "There ya go."

No surprise that "There ya go" also applies on the golf course. On a regularly-scheduled Saturday you and your buddies are partaking in a leisurely round and making decent time, completing the front nine in the recommended two hours. Eventually you catch up to the foursome ahead on the twelfth fairway. The members of this group who teed off nearly an hour ahead of you are each taking six or seven practice swings for every shot, then stroking it a miraculous seventy-five yards down range. They get to the green and start to plumb-bob their three-foot putts. They stalk the green from every angle like Tiger on the eighteenth at Augusta trying to win the Masters by a stroke. You want to bypass this detour but discover three more foursomes up ahead and realize that ain't gonna happen. Your easygoing, leisurely day has turned into a five and a half hour nightmare of a train wreck thanks to the foursome from Hell. Well, "there ya go."

At other times there are unexplained sounds that can be heard but their origin unknown. Occasionally historical facts and events can lead to their origin. Take the case of the wild, Wild West days of the 1800s, as exemplified by movie versions years later.

In the 1950s there were plenty of cowboy and Western type-movies on the big screen and many more on black and white television. In one particular movie, *The Bend of the River*, Arthur Kennedy, Julie Adams, and Hall of Fame actor James Stewart lead a wagon trail of about ten covered wagons through the desolate, arid areas of the old Wild West. This landscape included the wilderness west of the Mis'sip, which is how them cowboys and cowpokes pronounced "Mississippi" back then. I've always wondered if there was any difference between cowboys and cowpokes. Maybe the cowboys didn't poke the cows along, and were kinder and gentler to them. Maybe they were the forerunners of today's PETA (People for the Ethical Treatment of Animals) organization, along with their counter-organization "People Who Eat Tasty Animals." Maybe in not being poked with sticks, the cows actually responded in a more favorable way, moving along faster. The cowboys probably got the memo on this revelation, while the cowpokes did not. Today, the legend of the cowboy thrives thanks to several modern-day athletic teams named after them. The Dallas Cowboys, the Oklahoma State Cowboys, and the Wyoming Cowboys, just to name a few. On the other hand, the cowpokes didn't fare so well. I don't know of a single team name, town name, or tavern name called the "Cowpokes."

There is strong evidence that the cowpokes weren't real cowboys anyway. That is a possibility. If you go back and listen carefully to those old Western movies, you'll notice that the cowpokes were the ones hollerin' to the cows to "Get along little doggie. Yee-ha!"

"Doggie?" Sure, there was always one token shepherd dog helping to round up the herd—as if one dog alone could do this all at once? Maybe Lassie, but her show premiered much later than the cowboy shows, and besides, Lassie was a farm-kept dog that's main responsibility was to keep little Timmy out of the trouble that he found himself in every week. As that was a full time job, she couldn't venture into the outside world of the trail ride. No, these cowpokes made rookie mistakes in calling the herd of cows "doggies," as if they were oversized Great Danes or Greyhounds.

And it was the cowpokes who went into the saloons after a rough ride on the hot dusty trails at sundown and sauntered up to the bar to ask for a "shot of whiskey." They never went for a nice glass of spring water that the bartender kept behind the counter from the town's spring-fed well. Nope, always the whiskey. But what really separated the cowboys from the cowpokes was their barroom behavior. The cowboys hung around the bar for the evening sipping their shots of whiskey until Miss Kitty and her friends showed up. The cowpokes, on the other hand, not only downed their shots of whiskey but insisted on drinking the whole bottle and sat together at the saloon's tables getting drunk for the night. They would often get in bar fights for no apparent reason other than mistaken identity, or through trying to obtain another bottle of whiskey on credit. They used their advanced days allowance to pay in silver coins, carefully removed from their small leather pouches to defray the cost of the whiskey, never having enough money for a good evening meal or a second bottle. They always had to settle for the hardtack lunch on the trail the next day. Clearly, the cowpokes gave real cowboys a bad name. As a result, the cowpokes reputation has suffered to this day. No Old West stories, movie rights, or athletic team names to remember them by.

In *The Bend of the River*, Jimmie Stewart and his followers embarked on a slow journey through the countryside, attempting to mind their own business and stay out of trouble. They were headed west, though it was never explained why. They had probably heard Horace Greeley, the nineteenth century expansionist, shout the slogan, "Go west, young man!" And so they thought, "Okay, that sounds like a good enough reason for me."

In the early evening, before the sun had gone down over the western horizon, the wagons formed in a circle to gather 'round the campfire for warmth, for their protection—to ward off any predatory prairie animals like the wild packs of cay-oats, (coyotes to easterners), and to cook their vittles. They also had to heat some water for their ever-present coffee, which they apparently had plenty of since they tended to throw their cups down at the first sign of intrusion from Wile-E-Coyote.

At dusk was when the trouble started; at least it did in most movie versions of the *Wild Wild West*. As the women-folk heated up the night's dinner over the campfire, the men-folk patrolled the edges of the circular formation of the ten covered wagons, on the lookout for anything unusual. In the center of it all the kid-folk played "tag" and ran in circles, thanks to the circular boundary that contained them.

Through the stillness of the open prairie, as the women-folk served chow to the men-folk at the perimeter lookouts, the sounds of beautiful songbirds could be heard in the not-too-distant hills. "Those are the sweet sounds of birds calling," the women said. The distinctive bird tones *Caw, Caw, U-waaah, U-waaah* soon sounded much closer than before. "Aren't they beautiful?"

Jimmie Stewart, the wiser, more experienced, and more judgmental trailblazer, knew better than to trust these seemingly innocent sounds of the lonesome prairie. By pure instinct he realized the foreboding nature of the sounds—they weren't the type of birds typically found in that particular prairie desert. "The only birds out here at this time of day are buzzards, and they don't make sounds," he rationalized. "It must be Injuns."

Sure enough, before you could say "Geronimo," the first of many arrows flew closer than a knife-wielding circus performer popping balloons held steady by a maiden's mouth. Then, "swoosh," an unseen arrow nearly sent Julie Adams' hoop skirt flying right off her twenty-four inch waistline.

"Injuns! Here come the Injuns!" the men-folk relayed around the circular campfire as they tossed their tin cups of coffee to the ground.

To find out what happens next, you'll have to go to the archives and watch this enticing thriller, since I don't want to ruin the ending for you. It will be left to your imagination exactly how Jimmie Stewart and Julie Adams came to settle down right there at Prairie Junction, and establish the town central around that small campfire that saved their lives that night.

Similarly, when you hear the *Caw, Caw, U-waah, U-waah* of the birds chirping in the trees on a golf course but don't see any of the annoying offenders around, only one thought should cross your mind, "Must be Injuns." You will hear the sounds, but you won't see where the sounds are emanating from. Look around your perimeter, "Yup, must be Injuns."

If you're questioning how politically incorrect I am at this moment and want to go on the warpath (oops, he did it again), you must know that I am very closely associated with Native Americans and have the utmost respect for the Indian heritage. My wife of thirty-six years is part Cherokee, her father was half Cherokee, and his parents were Cherokee. Her family has been registered with the Cherokee Nation for many years, and her father, Jim, was part of the splinter group located in Arkansas, the North Carolina Cherokee Tribe. Now put that in your peace pipe and smoke it, all you tree huggers. If that isn't convincing enough, my younger brother Joe and I played "Cowboys and Indians" growing up, in the woods behind our house. And I was *always* the Indian.

"Surreal." Have you ever been a witness to anything surreal on a golf course? Naw, I didn't think so, and neither have I. But I hear this new-age word creeping into the everyday language of everyday Americans. "Hey man, I just saw a dog running down the sidewalk. Man that was so surreal." I think the people who overuse this word just want to sound sophisticated and use it to impress. "Hey, I ordered a latte with extra cream from Starbucks—it was so surreal." Oh, and the word is never delivered by itself—it has to be "so surreal," as though a simple "surreal" isn't enough for the listener. The more surreal it is, the more intense the situation. Betcha if you ask the person using the word if he or she knows the actual meaning, they wouldn't have the faintest clue. According to Merriam-Webster, for all you dictionary aficionados, it means, "very strange or unusual; having the quality of a dream." Also, "unbelievable, fantastic; synonymous with strange, weird, unreal, odd, dreamlike, bizarre." Now there you have it, all you surrealists. Try to adopt a different word the next time you describe an unusual event. There are no events in golf that are peculiar enough to be described as "so surreal." Fantastic, maybe; weird, yes occasionally; odd, most likely. This word must be banned from golf course language. Every course in the country should place a sign near the entrance to its clubhouse that calls for its banishment. The sign should display the word with a diagonal line through it, similar to the signs that prohibit dogs from walking on the lawn in parks.

According to vocabulary.com, "You see a bus crash into someone's front porch while a caged dog barks in the side yard, near a man in a business suit who is grilling hamburgers, you might call that a "surreal image." Things that are surreal combine unrelated elements to create a bizarre scene."

Okay, there ya go. Such an incident can be surreal and awesome, baby, at the same time.

Whatever happened to the exclamation: "You da man"? Let's bring this one back to tournament golf language. The pros don't exactly care for this one, but hey, you paid for the ticket to watch, did you not? It is your privilege to shout this at will so long as you don't disrupt another pro's backswing or, heaven forbid, Sergio when he waggles for the twenty-fifth time over the ball on a short pitch shot. This phrase has waned since big hitter and fan favorite John Daly has waned from most tournaments. Tiger Woods has somewhat waned from being in contention, and he too was "You da man"-worthy. In their honor, as long drivers of the golf ball, this phrase is reserved only for those big hitters off the tee, with averages of three hundred yards or more with the driver. So before you delve into "You da man" territory, do some homework first and then holler—*after* seeing that the ball has been smacked by one of the greats. May I suggest these fine players as your starter kit: Dustin Johnson, Gary Woodland, Rory McElroy, and Freddy Couples?

The term "Boom-shaka-laka" is acceptable, but merely on a restrictive basis, allowable once per nine holes, and only during your local round at a public course after smashing a huge drive that outdrives your partners (you know—the "Linda Rhondsat" type of drive, the one that "Blue Bayou"). You'll be feeling good about the game all of a sudden and will be justified in letting out a triumphant "Boom-shaka-laka!" with a chin up tilt of superiority. Generally your companions will smile, though perhaps snicker, but they'll love the enthusiasm. Guaranteed. The very next time you are outdriven by the sneerers, you will be getting the "Boom-shaka-laka" treatment back at you. Also guaranteed.

Variations of the "Boom-shaka-laka" are also frequently heard. "Ka-boom" is acceptable. The weird sounding "Ba-ba-booey" is an alternative catchphrase. Not sure where this one originated—some say it's from a radio personality. Even though it doesn't pertain to anything in the golf world, it still resonates.

Many of the phrases heard on golf courses and inside clubhouses are necessary, useful, and descriptive. But stay away from the trite phrases. I urge you to refrain from, "It is what it is." This phrase is heard from athletes, politicians, Hollywood celebrities, actors, actresses, and folks on the street. You might ask if this phrase is true, then the corollary is also true, "It isn't what it isn't." Guess that sums up nearly everything that can be discussed.

The true characters will say memorable things that will stick in your craw and remain in your craw for a very long time.

CHAPTER 6

Mr. D and "Boat"

WE CALLED HIM Mr. D, and he liked that name. He claimed it was the first time he had heard it, though I don't know if that is true or not—a man in his seventies can say these things that people often believe. We called him Mr. D mostly out of respect but also because we could not accurately pronounce his last name. I got to know him through George "Boat" Boatwright, my roommate in Hawaii, and my colleague, Roger Withrow, got to know him through me. George met Mr. D's daughter on Sunset Beach, and after a few weeks, we were both introduced to her dad, the golfer.

We were an improbable foursome that shared a love of golf and often started our Saturdays with the first tee time at 6:30 a.m., or "oh-six-thirty" military time.

Mr. D's name was Robert (Bob) Djidjitch. He pronounced his last name as "DidDitch" but with a "j" in the middle, so it sounded more like "Did-ja-ditch," said very quickly. He was an immigrant from the old country of Czechoslovakia, when it was still called Czechoslovakia. He came to the United

States after World War II after checking in at Ellis Island. Like the majority of hard-working European immigrants, he took up a trade in the tool and die industry in order to make a living and become successful. It wasn't clear to us if he specialized in tool or die cast; very doubtful that anyone could be a specialist in both categories. No one outside the industry knows exactly what a tool and die person does. I've never seen an ad requesting a need for a tool and die specialist anywhere in this country. Nevertheless, he was very proud of his career and past work with the tool and die industry, which later became the foundation for DuPont Industries in the 1950s, located in Chicago, Illinois.

Mr. D was a wealthy guy. How wealthy was never revealed nor asked about, but he owned a penthouse apartment on Lakeshore Drive in Chicago, a condominium in Boca Raton, Florida, and a one story ranch-style beach house on Sunset Beach, Hawaii. He liked to say these were his seasonal recreational homes, which he visited on a rotational basis each year. But he never really acted rich; in fact, he rolled his own cigarettes. He made it into a performance act when doing so, even believing that Clint Eastwood and Martin Van Cleve had copied him in the cowboy hit classic *The Good, The Bad, and The Ugly*. He used real tobacco, not the wacky, stinky weed that hippies in the Sixties and Seventies used to roll, and he used cigarette paper, the special kind just for cigarettes. He'd pull out his cigarette-making items after scoring his first par on the course, seal the end of the roll of paper with a lick down the edge, and light it. Then he'd take a puff and grin widely. It was an "I love this place" type of grin.

I've carried on his smoking tradition to this day, lighting up my stogie after my first par of the day. It continues to be my tribute to "A tradition unlike any other." Today my cigars have been premade and rolled by the factory, so it just comes down to chopping off the end for a better draw and lighting the other end. It is performed as a ritual and accompanied with an "I love it when a plan comes together," as uttered by George Pepard in the TV series *The A-Team*. We could have made our own "A-Team," with Mr. D as the Colonel. Even though he had never been in the military, he'd be in charge anyway. Other members of our A-Team would include George "Boat" as "Face," mainly because he was always scheming and thought he was the ladies' man; Roger Withrow as "Murdoch," because as an Army NCO, he pretty much knew how to get the unusual things done; and myself as "B.A.," not that I'm a body-builder or pro wrestler, but more because I'd want to rush in and take on projects way above my pay grade. And, I liked it when B.A. uttered distinctive phrases like "I pity the poor fool."

Boat was a friend of mine during our college years, and we've remained friends for more than forty years. We were both enrolled in the Army's ROTC program, and it was during our final semester of our senior year that we received our commission in the Army as Second Lieutenants. We also drew parallel first assignments. Our first written official military orders directed us to Fort Benning for Infantry Officer training, then on to Hawaii and the 25th Infantry Division. But first was three months of mostly outdoor training, exercises, and experience on the rifle ranges on the hot, nasty, sticky summer days among the southern Georgia pines. Neither one of us wanted to be in the Infantry, but if it meant a tropical island somewhere in the Pacific for three years, then we agreed to suck it up for a short while. Besides, for George, Fort Benning and Columbus, Georgia, were close to his home in Aiken, South Carolina, where he could retreat ever so often on weekends and holidays after training had been shut down. Boat was a pure southern-grown boy, with a corn-pone "how y'all doin" accent that he often used to his benefit with the young ladies he'd meet. They would go for it, too, not only because of his charming accent but because of his boyish natural looks with a lightly tanned cherub face. I would say the women were attracted to him. He tried hard to impress them as well with his tendency to laugh at their slightest bit of humor.

Boat and I ultimately linked up in Hawaii, on the extreme north shore tip of Oahu on the outskirts of small-town Haleiwa, where we rented a two-bedroom beach house together. The house was directly on the beach, nothing but fifty yards of sand between us and the Pacific Ocean waves. The property adjacent to the beach house colony was the Hawaii Polo Field and Club where England's Prince Charles and other celebrities would come to play. Polo tournaments were held there on the weekends as different Polo clubs would compete for fun and bragging rights, I assumed. These members already had the money to belong to the Club and to own their own horses, so it probably wasn't money they played for. We'd watch them, while leaning against the white fence line that separated our parking area from the field, close enough to see the chukkers chuck and to hear the shouts of the players, "Tally-ho, old chap," as they maneuvered their ponies over the open field.

On the opposite side of the road leading to our beach colony was a short, grassy airfield where single engine piper cub airplanes would pull air glider planes into the air. The gliders would softly return to the airfield after soaring around for thirty minutes in the gentle trade winds that were always swirling on the north end of the island of Oahu. A local native Hawaiian businessman owned the property and operated the planes that were part of the glider operation, mostly for his friends and the celebrities who wanted an adventure while visiting and playing polo on the weekends. It wasn't a tourist destination, as he didn't advertise his thrill ride. It was entirely due to word of mouth that people came to discover the airfield. Few tourists ventured out to the very end of the northwestern tip of the island, realizing there wasn't much else for tourists to see and do except for snorkeling or diving, which could be accomplished at other places around the island.

George and I tried it out one sunny, windy day. A casual trade wind was gently blowing across the island for ideal flying conditions. The two-person cockpit contained a trained operator working the controls in the front seat. George joined him up front while I sat in the rear. Whew! What a view we had as the glider was cut loose from the tow plane. We could clearly see the polo field down below, the crystal clear blue ocean for miles, and the Koolau mountain range as it rose up out of the water identifying the origin of the island from volcanic eruptions centuries ago. This was near the Kole-Kole Pass, the far end of the same stretch of mountain that the Japanese war planes came rumbling through to kick start the U.S. involvement in World War II in the Pacific. We didn't soar through the pass; it was too far away, and the downdraft winds of the mountain pass saddle would've taken the engineless plane down, smashing us into the rocks on the side of the mountain. We could see the cut of the Pass in the distance, close enough for me, and follow the outline of the mountain ridge that was covered in green with tropical foliage swaying in the ever-present breezes, as if waving "aloha" to skyward travelers.

Weekend adventures enabled us to experience the outdoor allure of the islands with abundant snorkeling, surfing, swimming, scuba diving, and golf.

At this point, Boat was a casual golfer and beginner just learning the simple aspects of the game, such as how to keep the ball in the same fairway he was playing. On one occasion on Oahu's Kalakaua golf course, his ball landed in the middle of an adjoining fairway where golfers were walking in the opposite direction toward us to their green, which was located behind us. A husband and wife duo was walking together on that fairway while pulling their walk-behind carts on that warm, pleasant, cloudless Saturday afternoon. They saw us and politely stopped about 125 yards away as we approached George's ball. Struggling to work his way back to our designated fairway, George smacked an iron that traveled smoothly and proficiently for a beginner, ascending five or six feet above ground level. Unfortunately, it was about 45 degrees off the intended line and was headed for the waiting couple. And *headed* it was, directly in line with the woman's skull. She instinctively raised her arms in order to protect her youthful face. The ball made a horrible cracking sound as it smashed into the woman's left wrist. Her gold wristwatch crumbled into small pieces, as if they were icicles that had been hanging from a tree limb and smashed by a hammer, pieces scattering to the ground in slow motion.

"Uh, oh, George. Looks like you broke her arm," I said.

"It wasn't intentional."

"I know, but you're in the wrong fairway."

"They waved us up to play," George weakly responded.

The couple shouted something inaudible to us as they approached. At that point we noticed the size of the guy she was with. I thought we had found Sasquatch right there in the middle of the island. He stood at least six-foot-four and appeared to be about 260 pounds, larger than the Incredible Hulk himself. We turned to each other as the thought of "fight or flight" came to mind. Flight sounded like the best option. But it was too late for that decision, and we figured the two of us could take on Bigfoot if we had to. It was time to apologize.

Our apology was interrupted by the big guy when he humbly announced, "Sorry for getting in your way, guys. Elizabeth is alright, only her watch was broken."

We offered to pay for the watch, but he declined. "See, Elizabeth? I told you to stand farther way," we heard him grumble as we rapidly raced-walked away from the near disaster.

Roger Withrow, one of the most avid, rabid golf lovers you could imagine was a career Army soldier. We were assigned to the same Army Transportation Company and were a team both at work and on the golf course. A country boy from Paducah, Kentucky, Roger had the down home charm that could persuade a leopard out of his spots. He was a calming voice in a chaotic, energetic military organization. He trained soldiers, supported and led them, and made them more proficient in their work. He sported light brown hair, cut in military close-ness, reddish complexion covering his white rounded face, and muscular arms with freckles. He often called me his 'lil brother whom, though I never met his actual brother, I sup-pose resembled his sibling of about my age.

As my golf mentor, he taught me the basics of the sport during our regular Saturday morning tee times at the military base. And it was Roger who cured me of my youthful hot-headed temper. One morning on the course, I slammed a driver into the ground, and later in the round, threw two clubs in a rage of disgust. Following this bout of poor behavior, he informa-tively said, "Do you know what your wild behavior looks like from across the fairway? Let me tell you. You remind me of an uncontrollable orangutan flailing away because he had his banana stolen from him. Besides, you're not good enough to get angry."

Roger and his family lived on the Army base within walk-ing distance to the nearest base golf course. He was a proud owner of a seven-year-old English bulldog, named Private Buford. He was saved from an animal rescue shelter, a victim of canine cruelty. Due to his size and breed, he was thrown into dog fighting rings. Unwilling to engage with the Pit Bulls and Rottweilers, he became the "punching bag" for training the fighting dogs.

"When we got him, his original name was Colonel Buford, but I had to change that," Roger quipped.

"Was that because he outranked you?" I guessed.

"That was part of it, but not the whole reason. When I called him 'Colonel,' his response was the same each time. He would only sit on his ass and bark at me."

Roger continued, "Private Buford is more energetic, fetches my newspaper, and responds to dog commands. He is more friendly and great with kids."

Private Buford is entertainingly unique as dogs go. He was once invited to a friend's wedding reception as the "Dog of Honor." Some of the younger children, to their delight, rode around the dance floor on his broadened back carried by short stumpy legs. A real party animal, he slurped a bit too much champagne that afternoon and managed to slump into a heap near the bride and groom's festive head table.

Private Buford has many allergies, too. He is allergic to cats and to grass, among other things. Because he can't go outside to chase the felines running through the neighborhood, he remains content to sit by the window and watch.

I introduced Roger to Mr. D at one of our Saturday morning golf outings.

Mr. D was fascinated by the idea of playing on a military base, and he eagerly accepted our invitation to join us. He hit the ball straight, but not far, and was a true ferocious competitor. He was feisty for a man in the twilight of life, and mentioned that he was a Golden Gloves Boxing Champion in younger days. When the years advanced, he taught boxing to aspiring pugilists. Mr. D retained his noticeable Slovakian-English accent. When he spoke, others around him listened intently. Having a five foot-nine slender physique, he had steely strong arms and a vice hold of a grip. He was a tough old nut with a quick wit and a soft heart.

After I had been playing exceptionally dismally for several holes to start my round, Mr. D leaned over from inside the riding cart and whispered in his raspy, crackled voice, "Pete, I know what your problem is."

"Oh, wonderful." I was hoping to get a quick lesson from the authoritative senior.

"You stand too close to the ball—after you hit it." Then came his signature throaty laughter, sounding like Donald Duck caught in a blender.

During the return trip to his beach house on the North Shore at Sunset Beach, he was intrigued by the pineapple fields and inquired about how the pineapples grew inside of each piney plant. Obliging his curiosity, I pulled off the main road and into the third row of pineapples where the compact car could barely be seen by the passing automobiles, and any security patrols, if there happened to be any roving the many square miles of the Dole plantation.

"Let's take some home," he insisted.

"No, Mr. D, we can't do that," Roger said, leaning forward from the back seat.

"Why not?"

"First off, it's a fifty dollar fine for each one taken, and they're almost impossible to chop off the prickly plant. We don't have anything to cut them with." Roger did his best to persuade him to look but not to touch.

We might as well have told a mule not to kick. Before Roger could finish his thoughts, Mr. D was tugging at the middle of the plant with his bare hands, grunting to get the lone pine-apple free from its habitat.

"These sonofbitches are rough," he said as he managed to extricate a prickly one from the stem rooted in the center of the plant. "How do you know which ones are ripe?" he asked. Without hesitating for a reply, he snapped off another, and another, which I quickly tossed into my car trunk. With our half dozen stolen fruits, we sped off through the fields with enough trailing dust and dirt to gain the attention of any Hawaii 5-0 investigator who may have been prowling nearby.

As I sped down the main island road passing the multitude of acres of pineapple plants, Roger and I surmised that this old geezer could have actually purchased the whole field with his millions. Now safely away from being discovered by the pineapple police, Mr D snickered like a schoolboy who had just gotten away with throwing spitballs at Joanie in the next row. Then he let out his Donald Duck imitation laugh.

After my first two years of golf in the beauty of the Hawaiian Islands, my three companions taught me lessons that I follow to this day. From a seventy-something year old, the lesson is to have fun and to adopt a devil-may-care attitude when taking calculated risks. From Boat, he taught me to stand up to ad-versity and to realize that the situation may not be as dire as it may seem. Finally from my old friend Roger, I learned to have good etiquette, to help those who need it, and that friendly advice lasts much longer than any round of golf.

And one more bit of advice, from Private Buford. Be humble and enjoy the people around you. Where's the next party?

CHAPTER 7

Colonel Brisbane

COLONEL BRISBANE WAS my senior rater when I was stationed in Heidelberg, Germany. In civilian terms, he was my
boss's boss, and I rarely got to talk to him or see him on a
regular basis. Maybe once per week, which was more than
sufficient, since frequent meetings with the senior guy usually led to more work tasks and therefore more opportunities
to screw up. He had a high level position in the Office of
the Deputy Chief of Staff for Personnel in the Headquarters
of the U.S. Army, Europe and Seventh Army. The Colonel,
with chiseled facial features, would win a staring contest with
Mount Rushmore. He was a very short man, although probably somewhat taller than a munchkin from the *Wizard of Oz*.
Perhaps a bit taller than a professional jockey, he was thin and
wiry, and was very aware of his stature.

In many ways, being short and slender in the Army may have
its advantages. Soldiers and officers must undergo an annual physical fitness- training test (APFT). The test consists of a
scoring system based on the number of push-ups performed
in two minutes, sit-ups performed in two minutes, and a

two-mile run that is timed for efficiency. Eight minutes per mile was considered a decent time, kind of average, but good overall. A person with a height disadvantage, it would seem to me, would enjoy an easier time with the push-ups since his arms are shorter than average and because he wouldn't have as far to push his body from the ground. Okay, maybe not "enjoy," but he'd definitely have an advantage. Similarly with the motion of a sit-up, since his torso is relatively shorter than a taller person's and he wouldn't have as far to move from the ground. Unfortunately, when running for two miles the shorter person would need to take more steps compared to the taller person, so that would be a slight disadvantage.

Even so, the Colonel was in excellent physical condition for a man of forty-two. He enjoyed playing handball and was often seen at the base gymnasium on the court during the noon lunch hour, getting in some daily physical activity. I guess handball is a short man's activity as well—he's able to quickly make contact with the low shots closer to floor level, and would seem to have a better angle to judge the trajectory of the ball against the forward and side walls.

At one of my senior rater to ratee discussions, Colonel Brisbane attempted to get to know me a little better—better than simply "that guy" working in the office under his supervision. After asking me typical questions about my personal background, family, friends, college education, hometown, and my relatively short military background of ten years, he began to ask some questions about sports. "Do you play handball?"

I noticed the corners of his mouth droop downward somewhat when I told him that I was no longer interested in the game. I had played some in college in an intramural league, and also played for fun at the previous bases where I had been assigned. I felt that the strategy of the game was exciting and the overall physical workout was extremely beneficial, at least more beneficial than the APFT. I was a decent handball player, but I wasn't crazy about the way both of my hands became reddened and puffy after smacking the ball for over an hour with padded gloves. And especially not crazy about the painful tingling I'd experience when the hard rubber ball would miss the palm of my hand and make solid contact with my fingertips.

"What about tennis?" he asked. "Are you a tennis player?" Aware that the Colonel enjoyed playing tennis as well as handball, I provided him with a brief explanation of my past experiences in the game of tennis. I experimented as a fresh-man when I was in high school, and during my junior and senior years I developed a decent game and climbed to the #4 position in singles. But it was a continual struggle to reach #3 or higher on the team. Matches in high school consisted of four singles matches and two doubles matches for a total of six matches, each representing one point in the overall outcome of the match. Our #1 singles player was also the valedicto-rian of the class for four years and was somewhat of a nerd. Our #2 singles player was also a nerd, as was the #3 player. Our coach, Mr. Jules Silverstein, was a teacher at our school whose primary job was to teach sophomore and junior level history courses. A man about forty, he was somewhat short and stocky, a friendly guy, but by all accounts a decent tennis player. He moved elegantly across the court while educating us on some of the game's finer points regarding strategy—very important to move properly in anticipation of the shot coming back across the net.

I particularly liked the competition as we competed for ranking on the team. I competed for the number three singles against one of our teammates, Billy Bochak. Billy was not much of an athlete, more of a cerebral player who understood angles, positioning, ball compression, swing rate, wind direction, arm length, and ratio, anything related to "E=MC squared." Much smarter than the average player, such as me. Despite our intelligence quota differential, we relished the competition and camaraderie that was our tennis team. He was a straight-A student who had been led into the game by Mr. Silverstein. During high school I was a good student and played other sports as well, which made me more of an athlete or jock rather than a nerd or bookworm like Billy Bochak. Frequently our matches settled down to the third set in a two out of three match, and the winner of the third set would be seeded either fourth or higher for singles on our team. Billy was also my doubles partner, since the third and fourth seeded players would be in the doubles competition. After high school, I played tennis at the college intramural level. In fact, during my four years in college I was considered the top #1 or #2 in intramural competition, all thanks to Mr. Silverstein and Billy Bochak.

I continued playing tennis recreationally wherever I was assigned during those years after college. My game improved as I became stronger, quicker, and more catlike on the court. Stationed in Missouri after college, I tried out for the All-Army tennis team and was selected for two consecutive summers. I was on top of my game and felt unbeatable until I met my nemesis, Second Lieutenant Quigley. Lieutenant Quigley was a member of my transportation truck company, assigned as a platoon leader and supply officer. "Quig," as everyone called him, was fresh out of the University of Oklahoma, where he ranked as the #2 tennis player for four years.

The challenge was raised almost immediately. Will the platoon leader of the company beat the Commander, or can the Commander top the younger, quicker, more talented tennis enthusiast? No one knew for sure if Lieutenant Quigley actually had a first name; he was always Quig to us. This was otherwise very rare and even unacceptable: everyone in the Army was strictly known as "last name, first name, middle initial." For those soldiers with no middle name, and therefore no middle initial, their profile was "last name, first name, no middle name (NMN)." Maybe Lieutenant Quigley's personal profile had read, "Quigley, no first name, no middle name" or "Quigley, NFN, NMN."

We played on Saturday mornings for the exercise, for the fun of it, and for the spirited competition. We formed a local tennis club with the assistance of several other tennis enthusiasts, and playing became a weekly event on our social calendars. Quig's youthful wife was also a tennis player and would occasionally join us on those Saturday mornings. "Liq" was also a recent graduate of the University of Oklahoma and played on the women's tennis team. Not sure if Liq had a first name either, as no one had ever heard it. Maybe Janet, Susan, or Harriet? No, it was only Liq. So it was "Liq and Quig," no first names, no middle names. Everyone who played against Quig was no match for him. He was much stronger and faster and could hit the ball harder than any of us. With his dirty blond hair and steely blue eyes, he looked like a Greek god about to harpoon us with his overpowering serve. The opposing player knew not to get too close to the net, lest he get

"Wilson" stamped on his forehead as an unwanted reward. After fulfilling his obligation to the Army, Quig resigned his military commission and returned back to his native state of Oklahoma to become a tennis pro at his local tennis country club. Liq and Quig made a fantastic tennis duo.

As he continued interviewing me, Colonel Brisbane learned that I enjoyed playing multiple sports, eventually realizing that my most enjoyment came from playing golf. He wanted to know if I would join in his foursome on Saturdays on the golf course in Heidelberg. "Of course it would be an honor to join in a casual round of golf at the local club," I said, jumping at the opportunity.

Within a few days the Colonel called me and asked me to join him and his colonel friends for a Saturday morning round of golf. "This is great," I thought. For the first time in my military career, playing on a social level may have its benefits with senior leaders. This could only result in a good outcome for my professional career. Or could it? At the very least the Colonel and I would get to know one another on a casual basis, without having to discuss any military business.

Upon approaching two of the other senior officers at the first tee, my nerves kicked in as my palms began to sweat, my legs began to shake, and my words came out in stutters. Thankfully, the Colonel cut me off and announced that he was interested in playing an internal golf game that he called "Bingo, Bango, Bungo," and asked if I was willing to join in this side game. Never having played the game before and not knowing what I was getting into, but wanting to be one of the guys in the foursome, I quickly agreed to join the game. I felt like I had signed a blank check and would find out how much the charge was afterward, and realized that perhaps it hadn't been a smart tactical move for me. On the other hand, agreeing quickly allowed me to be quickly accepted into the foursome. Not exactly a strategic *"Calculated Risk"* as described by the great four-star general of WWII, General Mark Clark, but it was my risk, nevertheless.

The Colonel then explained how his version of the game was usually played. Here's how it went: the term "Bingo" represented the golfer with the longest drive of the foursome and was worth one point toward the game. The term "Bango" represented the golfer who was able to hit his shot on the green first before the others in the least amount of strokes. "Bango" was also worthy of one point toward the total score. The term "Bungo" indicated the player who was able to put the ball in the hole before the other players. "Bungo" was also worth one point to the golfer who completed this task before the others. Each point of "Bingo, Bango, Bungo" was played for ten cents each; therefore, each golf hole had a combined total of thirty cents that a golfer could possibly earn. The grand total for eighteen holes of golf was a whopping total of five dollars and forty cents. As it would be very unlikely for anyone to receive every point on every hole for eighteen holes, I surmised that I could perhaps win a few dollars from the old colonels, or would have to surrender a few bucks in the course of our golf outing.

At the conclusion of the first full hole, the Colonel whipped out his scorecard and immediately added up the point value of our new game. Having out-driven the other three even in my state of nervousness (it was probably my adrenaline rush that made the ball fly so far), I was on the board already for the first point of our game. I had gotten the first "Bingo." Before we could walk off the green after the second hole, the Colonel whipped out the score sheet and quickly tallied up our points. "Colonel Johnson, you have the Bingo, I got Bango, and Colonel Swanson, you got the Bungo," he announced. Our golf game progressed that day in the same manner after every hole we completed. Colonel Brisbane the human calculator was very detailed in his description of who had won each point for each hole. At least we knew where we stood regarding our total points throughout the round, and the amount of money each golfer was to receive at the end of the eighteen holes was easily determined. I had enjoyed the day and was happy to have played a decent game, thinking to myself that I was finally making my way up the corporate ladder. Somehow I won a dollar and twenty cents that day, though I wasn't sure how many Bingo, Bango, or Bungo points it took me to do this.

The very next week, on Thursday, Colonel Brisbane called me and asked if I wanted to join his foursome again that upcoming Saturday. "Yes, of course, I would like to play again," I said, and expressed my appreciation for the invitation. The same foursome, the same golf course, the same tee time and of course the same game of "Bingo, Bango, Bungo" was to be played. After each golf hole was played out, the Colonel again displayed his scorecard and tallied each point that each golfer had acquired. The Colonel was on a mission and he was tenacious in totaling each person's score, especially our side game accounting. Although a lover of the game, he was not a particularly good golfer and, for the most part, he was outdriven by everyone on each fairway. However, his strength and strategy was to get the ball in the hole before we could.

He probably had more "Bungo" points than anyone else.

The following week he called me again on Thursday and requested that I play another round of golf that Saturday. Not wanting to disrupt our camaraderie at that point, I agreed on one more time. Again, it was "Bingo, Bango, Bungo" as the human calculator added up the scores immediately following each golf hole. This routine of requesting my appearance each week on Thursday, playing on Saturday and of course "Bingo, Bango, Bungo" each time continued for the next four weeks. Now, there was no backing out of this. We realized that for one of the members of the foursome to refuse to play the points game was gravely offensive to the Colonel and akin to usher in World War III.

Colonel Brisbane insisted on continuing this nutty game, which was comparative to eating a medium rare steak every week. A thick, succulent steak can be special, but how special can it be after eating it week after week? This is what "Bingo, Bango, Bungo" became, the same tired steak meal renewed week after week. After three summer months of Saturday golf, I devised a plan to excuse myself from the foursome.

"Colonel, I'm taking the family on a Volksmarch in Sweitzegen this weekend. No golf for me."

"Volksmarches are two day events. You can go either Saturday or Sunday," he retorted. Dammit, I couldn't escape the guy.

The following week, I tried this approach—"Colonel, I don't feel too well. Feels like a head cold coming on."

"You'll be okay in a few days, be sure to get some rest and drink plenty of fluids."

Finally, the clincher—"Colonel, my wife says if I play golf again this weekend, she'll leave Germany."

"Well, then—you'll have more time to play!" This is what I imagined he would say, but he did not.

"Humph, okay. I'll get someone to fill in," is what he did say.

"Free at last, free at last, Gawd almighty free at last." I'm sure I wasn't the first to utter those words to myself, but they sure fit the situation.

Finally liberated from the grasp of the insipid "Bingo, Bango, Bungo," I reflected on my hypothesis that socializing with the boss would have positive results. Golf is fun, but "Bingo, Bango, Bungo" is not fun when played endlessly. As for cozying up to the boss after a summer's worth of golf—that never became a reality. He submitted the worst report card I had ever received on my military record. Doubtful that Colonel Brisbane liked losing small amounts of money each week, or maybe he thought my excuse to leave the group was weak. Perhaps he took it personally.

Everyone should learn from this. President Barack Obama and Speaker of the House John Boehner recently played some friendly rounds of golf together in order to discuss issues of national importance. They were supposed to discuss, and perhaps agree on, things like the national debt, unemployment, jobs, and bank bailouts. They managed not to solve anything, and only came away as more unfriendly toward each other's political party. The newspaper accounts said that it was possible that Mr. Boehner refused to play "Bingo, Bango, Bungo" with the Prez. Same thing happened with the Colonel and me. Allow me to golf with these politicians so that I can help solve the country's problems. I'd tell them what's really happening down here in mid-America land. I might even take a few bucks from them during "Bingo, Bango, Bungo."

CHAPTER 8

Harry, Doc, and the General

IT WAS ONE of those days when I needed to work on my driving. My buddy had beaten me by three strokes the past weekend, and now he was feeling like Arnie all of a sudden. His facial features and body posture actually resembled Jason Dufner, but he was playing like Joe the Duffer. Joe the Duffer rarely beats me, but lately he's been climbing the personal leaderboard. For our next golf adventure, we put a steak dinner on the line. "Steak, loaded baked potato, salad with vinaigrette dressing, bottle of burgundy wine, and a decadent desert with ice cream ala mode," he clamored. Not just any old steak, he scowled, so game on.

It was a quiet, drizzly, not quite-raining-yet overcast day, and I was the lone figure on a 20-station driving range at Kiln Creek Country Club in Virginia. With a very large, el Grande, bucket of balls, the amount it would take two hours to go through if they were spaced out ten seconds apart, I was working on perfecting my drives. Not exactly perfecting, more like correcting a boomerang hack of a horrendous slice that crept into my bag somehow over three weeks ago.

That was the last time I edged out Joe.

After over an hour of slicing, whiffing, and grounding into double plays, I tried to remember the tips given out nightly on the Golf Channel. At that point I could've used an hours' worth of help from the 2012 Mr. Instructor of the Year, Michael Breed. My drives were down from 250 yards to 240 yards at most. That's 210 out and a minimum of thirty yards wide right. Frustrating. But at least there was no one there to witness this, within listening range of "son of a b**, stupid a@***#," muttered under my breath, but loudly enough for my ears. Psychiatrists believe that self-talk is good for the soul, and that people who talk to themselves are more productive than those who do not talk to themselves. How much longer do I have to wait for the productive part to kick in, I wondered?

From the side of the range near the well-trimmed bushes that lead down a small hill, I heard a voice telling me, "You're swinging from your heels."

A nicely groomed gentleman wearing a forest green polo shirt, khaki pants, and no golf hat approached me, tugging a pull cart behind. Seemingly from out of nowhere in the misty gloominess, like Will Smith in the *Legend of Bagger Vance*, Harry offered his tip o' the day: "You have too much weight on your heels."

"Okay." Fulfilling my New Year's Resolution of reducing chit-chat with strangers on the course, I kept my reply short, but not curt.

"Here's what *I* want you to do," he continued. "*I* like the way you approach the ball from behind, visualizing your target. But you step toward the ball directly behind it. *I* want you to come from a wider angle from the left, like this."

"Hmmm... okay."

"And tee the ball up lower. This allows you to swing through the ball more readily."

"Okay."

"Now, move seventy percent of your weight to the balls of your feet, not the toes. The balls of your feet, like this."

"Okay, got it."

"Now make three practice swings without addressing the ball," he instructed. So I did.

"That looks good; how does it feel?"

"Much better, I see what you mean. I'm trying lots of different things to fix this darned slice," I explained.

"Practice moving toward the ball from a wider angle, tee it lower, place seventy percent of your weight on the balls of your feet, and do this each time."

I started doing what Helpful Harry suggested. He then asked, "Can I borrow two range balls to hit? I want to loosen up before getting in five or six holes before heading home."

"Sure Harry, here you go."

He walked over to the edge of the range, teed it up, and took an elegant swing. The ball crashed wildly to the right and over a clump of bushes in the direction from which he arrived earlier. His second shot was even uglier, hit cloud high and whirled nearly 90 degrees right from the range, over the bushes and hills, into the far right rough of hole #1. From the edge of the range he disappeared into the mist as though vaporized by the enveloping, graying afternoon.

For the next hour, I butchered range balls attempting Harry's instruction. My slice had been cured, but I wasn't sure about Harry's game. Feeling much improved, I headed off to an away game in southern New York State.

At Spook Rock Golf Course, a beautifully manicured and terrific layout tucked in the southeast corner of New York State, the starter hooked me up with Nick, another single, and two others, David and his wife, Margi, who were paired as partners. Spook Rock, named after an Indian legend in which wicked spirits were diverted from harming the local Allegheny Tribe on account of a large granite stone, was some time ago named the best public course in all of New York. It is owned and maintained by the Town Of Ramapo. The starter himself, Tommy, although not from the Tribe, is legendary. A starter and local icon for many years, Tommy told me about his days with the 82nd Airborne Division in Ft. Bragg, North Carolina. After learning that David, the oldest gentleman in our foursome, was once a physician in the Army, now currently a full time civilian doctor, and about my time in the Army as well, Tommy eagerly joined in our military conversation. On that particular summer day, I was sporting my newest pieces of apparel, a U.S. Open hat with a Pinehurst logo and a skin-caressing moisture-wicking golf shirt I obtained from my stint at Pinehurst #2. Glancing at my apparel, Tommy recalled how he and his fellow Airborne Company had accidently parachuted onto the Pinehurst Golf Course, located many miles south of the intended landing zone at Ft. Bragg. The entire 75-man company was scattered all over the resort like marbles on a kid's playground, each not aware of his exact landing location, having drifted where the winds decreed. Tommy managed a perfect 10 (all ten toes on the ground) that was smack in the center of the green on hole #10. "First time I ever arrived on the green in regulation," he snorted and laughed simultaneously.

"You can leave the extra cart here," he instructed. "Four of you don't need three carts. We economize here, this ain't like the Federal Government in Washington."

"Yea, leave it right here, I'll take care of it, I'll make it happen," added Tommy, the gentleman starter.

Now that's a true military response from a former soldier. "Airborne!" I shouted back at him in his starter shack perch, emphasizing the "Borne" as is customary within Army jargon.

With military precision, we began our game at 8:06 a.m. Unfortunately for Nick, this also describes his left-right-left directions regarding the golf ball. Turns out that Nick is, and was, a military man with over twenty-eight years in the military, devoting time to each of the services. A Reservist, he finished his career with the Air Force, logistics mainly, and was promoted to Lieutenant Colonel. He then joined the New York State Militia in order to remain connected to the men and women in uniform. An *Italiano* from the Bronx, Nick Silvio is sixty-four years of age but doesn't appear to be thanks to his dark, tanned skin and neatly combed jet-black hair with its few gray specks. His impeccably-groomed hair never had a thread out of place during the four hours we played, despite the gentle breezes blowing through those hills.

At the turn, the threesome playing behind us stopped to complain to the starter about something we couldn't hear. They were pointing toward us, idling in our carts outside the snack bar waiting to head to the back nine.

I said to Nick who was sharing our cart, "Looks like those guys are complaining about something."

"Well, let them complain to me. I'll make one phone call, and *my boys* will be here to take care of it. They'll never complain again."

Where was I? Suddenly and without warning we had landed in the middle of a *Sopranos* episode. His real brothers, Philly, Geno, Louie, and Tony are all city employees of New York City. Nick had retired less than three months ago with the City Sanitation Department, ending as a main supervisor there with one hundred fifty employees under him. And what about Tony, living in New Joisey? I was afraid to ask.

Later on in the round, one of the three strangers in the cart behind us continued to edge near us on several successive greens. "I don't like when guys push us, and get too close behind," Nick emphatically stated. "If they keep it up or say something to us, I'm calling *my guys*. They will be here in minutes. They all like me and we take care of each other."

He meant it, and I believed it. In the middle of the eighteenth fairway, he took out a small metal flask containing a strong-smelling liquid. "I forgot that I still had some Jack Daniels in here. This has honey in it and tastes real smooth. Here, take a few sips."

This was a test, of that I was certain. It was time to show allegiance to *The Family*. Sure enough, it was either Philly, Geno, or Louie watching from the parking lot stationed on top of the hill from the eighteenth green. Probably not Tony, though, as he rarely got directly involved. He typically sent his Lieutenants to do the job. At least in the TV show, that's what happened.

The Jack Daniels went down smoothly, thanks to its lightly sweetened taste and pleasantly warm sensation. It felt good and right to be a part of *The Family*.

My second stop during the summer heat of July was at the Phillip J. Rotella Memorial Golf Course in Rockland County, New York. Named after a prominent county politician, the course boasts a remarkable layout situated near the towns of Thiells and Mount Ivy. Located on a meandering country road, it's a few minutes off the Palisades Interstate Parkway that connects New York City and upper New Jersey with rural New York State. Only thirty miles from downtown New York City, it has entertained many important political leaders, television personalities, professional sports figures and other celebrities on day trips from the big city. I was paired up with none of the biggest names from the Big Apple but with a well-known local guy, "Doc." Joining us that day was Ted Mathewson, a vacationer from North Carolina, who came to New York for some sightseeing, and a golf getaway.

Ted was a pleasant soul, middle-aged, friendly to talk to with a soothing sound of his voice. He had an air of serenity and calmness around him throughout the day. He talked in a low, mostly inaudible tone even when standing directly in front of him, or next to him with my good ear, my left one, leaned toward him only a few feet away, he could hardly be understood. Most of the day I simply smiled and nodded to him about whatever he was saying. He never dreamed of raising his voice, not even for a wild or chunky shots he had often made. It was like he was silently keeping a secret and did not want to reveal it to anyone, let alone to a stranger like me who he'd met only minutes ago. This *golf whisperer* was as stoic and stone-faced as former football Coach Tom Landry was on the sidelines of a Dallas Cowboy football game.

Forever the wise guy, I tried to get his ire up by mentioning various topics unrelated to golf.

"Ted, what do you think about all the illegal immigrants coming into our country from the southern border?" I quizzed.

"Well, they just needed someplace to go, I assume," was his monotone answer.

"Ted, how do you feel about all the defects on these new automobiles, especially the airbag recalls?"

"The industry will sort it out" he replied. No inflection in his voice or any reaction.

"How do you feel about the higher taxes here in the northeast and these toll roads everywhere?" Certainly that would shake him up.

"Glad I'm just visiting here for a short time," he said in a whisper.

As the game progressed, I put one of my drives way out of bounds with a banana slice. "Sonofabitch, damned slice

I thought I got rid of on the driving range," I shouted and choked the grip of my driver to death waiving it in the air over my head. All those antics couldn't bring back that well-used Titleist, and we all knew it.

"Sorry, guys," I apologized for my outburst. "I got carried away."

It was right then that I remembered that Ted Mathewson was an Ordained Baptist Minister from Cary, North Carolina. It was incongruent how this soft-spoken, quiet man could be a Baptist Minister from the Bible Belt. Although I'm not a Baptist, I've seen movies and heard stories about how Preachers bellow out their weekly Sunday sermons to the congregation. "ALLELUHAH, AND AMEN I SAY. CAN I GET AN AMEN!" and of course the churchgoers in the pews shout back, "AMEN."

I felt I owed the Minister an immediate confession about my four letter words stated with hatred and anger toward the innocent white golf ball. Baptists don't confess their sins the way Catholics do, in a darkened phone booth sized confessional box. Only the priest needs to hear the dreadful sins of the confessor, in which the sinful has to carry out a pocketful of silent prayers or good deeds administered to his fellow sinners.

Baptists shout out their misgivings inside the chapel for the entire church attendees to hear and to prayerfully forgive the sinner. Either way, sins are resolved or God forgives the human wrongdoing. "Amen." The question becomes, though, how are Ministers and Priests forgiven if they can't confess to others in the same proceedings allotted to parishioners?

You may have heard about the Baptist Pastor who skipped Sunday morning service on one beautiful summer day. He played hooky with an excuse that he wasn't feeling all that well and up to delivering the normal hour or longer sermon. He went to the golf course instead, alone.

During that morning, he was playing the best golf of his life when an angel observing from above asks God, "Are you going to let this slide? Do something! You are God!"

So God says, "Watch this."

The Pastor hits a 425-yard tee shot and the ball goes in the hole for a double eagle. The angel asks, "Why did you reward him?"

God replies, "Who is he gonna tell?"

Unfortunately Doc, the third member of our group, was not a real doctor, as I was hoping to get some free medical advice for my ailing lower back and occasional neck pain. Doc is a government contractor employee who travels to the four corners of the world to solidify new contracts with foreign corporations. The very next day, he'd be off to Thailand and then to Singapore for that very reason. From Mount Ivy to the exotics, all with clubs in hand. Oh, the stories he told about the grandeur and excitement of traveling through Mount Ivy to speak with the peoples of Southeast Asia. As one fable goes, the notoriety of Mount Ivy was once the central point of old-time comedian and actor Charlie Weaver. Charlie, with floppy bucket style hat, whitish whiskers and mustache, often told of his charming small town USA, Mount Ivy. However, Charlie had never set foot in the area. On his travels from New York City to the Catskills entertainment resorts, he saw the sign directing parkway traffic off the exit ramp to Mount Ivy, and thought what a nice, quaint way to perfect his comedic act. I offered this background to my playing companion for the day, Doc.

Doc had the look of a *Crocodile Dundee* character in the movie of the same name. Although a bit older than the original Mick Dundee, he wore a leather bush hat squashed down over his tanned, leathery face. I was expecting him to pull out a two foot long bush knife from his cargo pants pocket and declare "Now that's a knife." He sure could've used a machete like that as he found himself hunting for the balls he caromed into the high brush well off the fairways. Maybe he was hoping to find snakes or wild beasts, where he was looking. His golf swing mirrored a downward chop, chop with clumps of grass flung high and forward after every stroke. He was truly golf-swing challenged. But Doc enjoyed the hunt. Riding in his own cart, he rapidly drove ahead of everyone's shot and pointed to where the ball had come to rest. Like a purebred Bloodhound or English Pointer, he was helpful and annoying at the same time.

Donald O. Cochran didn't care much for his first given name and wouldn't reveal his middle name, so it must have been equally hideous to him. He was just D.O.C. Doc was trying to be helpful, more so than the three teenagers in a later episode who challenged the Commanding General at the Pines, military golf course on Fort Eustis, Virginia.

The three teenage hooligans played verrrry slowly in the group just ahead of the two-star Major General and his playing companions, a one-star Brigadier General and two senior ranking Army colonels. The young beginners seemed undaunted by their surroundings as they whooped it up, looked for lost balls and drove around in circles, holding up the foursome behind them. The two-star general, the Commander of the Army post and the high-ranking official in the Department of Defense Transportation System, was a Saturday regular with a standing tee time. Tee times were vacant immediately before and after this starting time so the foursome could breeze through in order to keep to their busy schedule. The group of teenagers began clowning around on the second hole, requiring the Commander and his buddies to wait to hit every shot after they'd been on the course for barely fifteen minutes. In an attempt to speed up play, the general hit his ball over the pond on hole #5 to the par 3, which landed within a few feet of the young group lining up their putts. This happened to be the third time the general's golf ball had landed near the boys.

Without hesitation, one of the boys picked up the beautifully aimed shot and heaved it into the pond surrounding the green. In an instant, the enraged general arrived at the scene, bewildered at what he had witnessed.

"That was my ball you tossed into the water," General Fielder breathlessly shouted.

"Yeah, dude, it landed on my green and too close to my buddy putting for his double bogey. You messed up his stroke."

"Do you know who I am?" an astounded General Fielder asked, without waiting for any response. "I am commander of this post, so by technicality, this is *my green*."

"Yeah, and I am General Patton," came the quick-witted reply of the gum-popping, fuzzy-faced teenager with a give-a-shit attitude.

It didn't take long for the two MP's (Military Police) to arrive and escort the ne'er-do-wells off the general's course. Too bad for General Fielder, now visibly shaken, who returned to the teeing area to redo his tee shot, conforming to USGA rule 904.2b(a-7), sub-paragraphs 13 ,14 . His reconstructed shot was chunked and landed in the pond, very near the watery grave where his earlier ball had splashed down thrown from the teenage punk. From a probable birdie to a double bogey, totally caused by impatience and a non-conforming trio of youngsters. The general became more annoyed and flustered when he was reminded that the kid he almost hit had also carded a double bogey on the "General's Hole."

What once was a scummy green, lifeless one-third acre of a watery hindrance surrounding hole #5, has since turned into a home for numerous water-loving creatures of nature. Frogs leap from its edges, turtles sunbathe on rocks and logs, ducks abound, and the Canadian geese that never return to their northern homeland have all claimed the pond as their rightful place. Management turned the golf ball graveyard into a waterfowl oasis with the addition of a water fountain in its center. The fountain adds cleanliness and soothing freshness to the beauty of the 175-yard looming disaster of a golf hole. The fountain shoots a cascading twelve-foot high plume of water from the epicenter of the enclosed pond which sends rippling waves to the outer edges. The pipe system that sucks in the water like a whirlpool drain makes a low grumbling gurgling sound much like someone gargling mouthwash in the morning hours. To most casual players passing by, that's the sound being heard. To members who play the course repetitively, they believe what they are hearing is quite different. If you listen intently, you can hear what they say the fountain's apparatus is proclaiming: *General's Hole.*

CHAPTER **9**

Gadgets

GOLFERS ARE ALWAYS looking for ways to improve their swing and lower their scores. With all the new developments in modern technology, a golfer has the unwritten guarantee from manufacturers that their products will improve his or her skills. These new training devices will help to "improve distance by five yards or more," "improve accuracy off the tee by ten percent," "maintain better stability and balance," and "increase power," not to mention achieve "greater consistency." Hmmmm, let's see; a better golf ball gives you five to ten more yards, accurate irons give another five more yards, a high speed lightweight multi-composite metal driver with a club head the size of a watermelon guarantees ten more yards to out-drive your buddy, new shoes give better balance and controlled body movement, adding another five yards; newer, softer club grips will outperform others by ten yards, tees with brushes on the top give less resistance and at least five additional yards, the rangefinder will lower your score and, finally, a new golf bag will make you look and play better.

Thanks to these vast improvements, you are now driving the ball 380 yards and right down the middle every time, aren't you? You more than doubled your distance on your drives and corrected that ghastly slice, and suddenly shooting under par, your handicap is near zero. You have new, better friends too. Your old friends now hate you because you have embraced technology and now look more like a pro, at least in appearance. It's not your fault that they didn't take out a second mortgage in order to pay for all these gadgets to fix their games for the simple pleasure of additional yardage.

But beware of many of the newer upgrades to the clubs you choose. For example, titanium-coated golf clubs can create fire-producing sparks when they graze rocks, an actual scientific study has found. After fires broke out at two Orange County California golf courses—the one at the Shady Canyon Golf Club in Irvine burned twenty-five acres and came close to taking out a few houses—county fire investigators could find only one common factor associating the two fires.

"Each golfer had used titanium-plated three irons at the course before the fire," said Orange County fire authority Captain Steve Concialdi. "The ground was rocky on the courses and, while everyone was wary of that conclusion, it was the only solution we had." I'm thinking Shady Canyon's previous name of "Rocky Canyon" was better suited to it. But, then again, those who value their lives might not want to venture out to "Rocky Canyon Country Club," particularly the locals.

There were other theories about the wildfires out West, so the fire investigators enlisted the help of scientists at the University of California-Irvine. These scientists had recently finished an eight month long study that resulted in a name change from "Global Warming" to the more hip moniker of "Climate Change." You can thank them for this, not to mention the government grant they received to switch over to the more modern 21st century name of "Climate Change." Now mostly idle, this team of crack scientists had little to do except for maybe cleaning out the petri dishes once filled with Ebola viruses, which they had dropped on the floor in all their excitement over deciding upon a new name for the miniscule increase in temperature over the past fifty years of climate study. They are currently working on a proposal for a government subsidy funded by the taxpayer to find an updated, more pleasant-sounding name for "Beach Erosion."

Researchers recreated, in the lab, the conditions of the courses where the fires started. Really, they did. They couldn't just walk out the back door of the three-city-block-sized laboratory to the first tee at Shady Canyon to conduct their observations with real golfers and real titanium-laced clubs. They even embedded rocks from one of the sites into the simulated ground at the lab for the study. Well, at least they managed to use real rocks and not environmentally-approved ones. They also used high-speed video cameras and powerful microscopes to capture the effects of striking or grazing the ground with the titanium club versus a steel one. While the steel club did not produce any sparks, the titanium club was a different story.

"After striking the rocks with the titanium club, we observed sparks that registered three thousand degrees and lasted one second," said James Earthman, a chemical science professor at UC-Irvine and the lead researcher on the study. His pal and assistant, Joe Spaceman, did not participate in the study. His area of expertise happens to be golfing on the moon's surface, which he has been researching ever since Neil Armstrong hit a moon rock with his 9-iron back in 1969. He's still trying to figure out why dust flew up into Neil's space helmet and obscured his vision after he dislodged a rock. The second moonwalk, by astronaut Buzz Aldrin, was undertaken to retrieve the very rock struck by Neil Armstrong, since he was unable to see it and grab it with all the dust flying around.

"If that spark had reached dry foliage, it would've ignited almost instantly," Earthman said. Absolutely true, as could a bolt of lightning, a leftover campfire, or a smoldering cigarette flicked out of a car window by some uncaring, non-environmentally conscious traveler (from out of state, no doubt). Californians would never commit such a dastardly deed; they've all attended Chief Billy Bob's "Fire Safety and Prevention at Public and Private Facilities" course.

While most golf clubs have steel heads, Earthman said that titanium alloys are used in some clubs because they make them lighter and easier to swing, especially when chipping balls out of tough spots. Hell, my friend T. Foster could have told him that. He has lots of practice chipping out of tough spots every time he plays. While those titanium-coated clubs are fine away from dry areas, when they graze small rocks, they can cause fire. "I've seen small sparks fly off my own titanium driver," Earthman said.

Then why all the fuss over conducting this massive research project if you already knew that sparks fly from your own titanium driver? Earthman, you could have asked T. Foster the same question and he would've told you that we both have seen sparks fly from his driver as it makes contact with the rocks near his ball. It doesn't take a rocket scientist to understand this. Oh, wait—Earthman is not a rocket scientist, after all. He is a material science scientist.

Believe it or not, the study was published in the journal *Fire and Materials*. The study would've been more complete if they had taken two minutes to interview T. Foster.

Marty Maciaszek, director of communications at the National Sporting Goods Association, said the group has rarely heard about the titanium-coated clubs causing sparks. Marty, don't lose any sleep over this. T. Foster hasn't—in fact, he is somewhat fascinated by it and wants me to swing his club as he tries to light his cigar while crouching near the rocks. We both believe that three thousand degrees ought to do it—or do the UC-Irvine scientists need to get more money to study the phenomenon? Our hypothesis would be as follows: "Can tobacco leaves, when rolled into cigar-like shapes and smoked on the ground by T. Foster, be ignited by the sparks created by the titanium-coated club that I swing against a rock?" We would need part of that government grant, thank you, maybe fifty percent of it since we (and by "we" I mean T. Foster) is assuming all the risk of being set on fire. Maciaszek said that while organization officials are still gathering information, they obviously urge golfers to be as cautious as possible. Okay, I'll be sure to let T. Foster know, and we won't forget the fire extinguishers next time out.

Only in California would scientists spend time and money to study the effects of hitting a golf club against a rock. Some interesting yet troubling ideas come from that state.

To help offset the cost of research the State of California charges a tax surcharge to play golf there. They refer to it as a luxury sports tax. The officials are blaming golfers for the state's 950 annual wildfires, too. They now require all golfers to carry a portable red fire extinguisher in their bags, roughly the size of a foot-long sub sandwich, issued and rented at each clubhouse for an extra fee. Under Fire Ordinance 675.6, section 14b of the California Fire Code, your clubs must be registered with the local Fire Chief as potential lethal fire starters. To register before your round of golf, you pay another substantial fee for the registration and accompanying bag tag stating that your clubs have undergone a thorough annual statewide certified inspection. Prior to receiving your official documents allowing your lethal weapons on the California courses, you are required to take a forty-hour course on "Fire Safety at Public and Private Facilities" offered quarterly by the State's Department of Fire Prevention, Wildfire Authority and Management Office. Only this office, and I emphasize, *only* this office can authorize wildfires within the state, according to their official-sounding title. After paying the fee for this mandatory training course, you are free to tee it up anywhere in the county in which you received the training.

If you choose to venture outside that county (Orange County for example, because this is where the initial fire-starting evil-doers were found at fault), you are required to take the local county refresher training and, of course, pay that county's fee. Golfers take note –this is *not* a tax—no, this is a fee and there is a difference. This is due to the fact that Orange County already has the highest effective tax rate in the entire country, so citizens have banded together to demonstrate against any additional taxes placed on them. For verification, just ask "Linda the Liberal," my sister Anne's longtime friend.

"Nosiree, no additional taxes here, only a fee for the right to play your luxury sport." Incidentally, the second and third highest tax rates in the U.S. are charged by Rockland County, New York and Nassau County on Long Island, New York. However, New York doesn't charge any additional fees for golf, presumably because there aren't many wildfires in that part of the country and so there's not an urgent need to educate players on the hazards of fire endangerment and on fire prevention. Instead, public officials encourage all course pro shops to display a larger than life, ten-foot cardboard cutout of Smokey the Bear wearing a menacing growling expression and carrying an oversized shovel—one that he'll whack you over the head with if you even think about starting a small campfire in the state. New Yorkers understand straight talk, and when Smokey says he'll whack you, that's exactly what he means. Whether he does it himself personally behind the cart barn or hires his cousin Yogi, you don't need to know the details, only that violators will be prosecuted to the fullest extent of the law after Smokey takes his turn.

Enhancements to equipment and golfing techniques are advertised everywhere. A recent edition of *Golf Magazine* offers enticing tips in the article, "How to be a Birdie Machine: The New Rules for Splitting Every Fairway, Hitting Greens, and Draining Every Putt." Read this article and you'll be playing just like Justin Rose. Another edition reveals how to "split every fairway—drive it straighter than ever with my five secret moves." Absorb these secrets if you'd like to play like Adam Scott. Or you can also "Steal Tiger's Power Move—The New Secret to Impact." I couldn't stop myself from diving into these articles, especially the first one, because I really, really want to be a "birdie machine."

The inside page opens strong with "the #1 ball played at the U.S. Open, 66 years and still counting, the Titleist." So, I got a dozen of the Pro V1, but stayed away from the Pro V1x. I associate anything labeled with an "x" with the "xxx'd" out balls my friends and I started with. They didn't go very far, except into the woods, and when hit out they always appeared to be smiling. On the opposite page the ad contains pictures of twelve pro golfers in various stages of their swings. None of them are smiling—they're mostly grimacing, probably at the fact that they just hit a five dollar golf ball into the woods or water hazard. Very clever, you Titleist advertisers, conveying a subliminal message through the image of the twelve golfers, each representing one of the dozen golf balls in the box. To get the full benefit of this ball, you are encouraged to join "Team Titleist" on their web page. I wonder if they give out team jerseys with "Titleist" scribbled on the front. Your number should be printed on the back, which would be your current USGA handicap. I'd consider joining if they'd make me the leadoff hitter on every tee.

Next page, next improvement. "Callaway, the top driver tested in its class. Excels in all performance categories." From the *Golf Magazine* Club Test, 2014. "Big Bertha named best in class by *Golf Magazine*... You can't argue with physics." Maybe not, but you can argue with the Physics teacher. Like if gravity keeps you weighted down on earth, why does water do the opposite when you are submerged and tries to push you up? Why doesn't gravity exist in the water, since all the oceans in the world manage to stay put?

Next up, the Rolex watch, and it's not just any old watch, no, of course not. "This watch has seen golf's most comprehensive tests. And the game's most rewarding victories." Intriguing to say the least, but my twenty-two dollar Timex has the same quality. It has been with me on the couch as we watched the same victories on television. And watched them in high definition. Can the Rolex claim that? I didn't think so. No claims to improve your game, but you will look good in this watch while you chop out of the ankle-high rough. With its gleaming gold inner band and golden ring around the bezel, you will be beaming lasers from the sun forward to your friends who have reached the green. You'll never be out of range thanks to the crowning achievement that is the Rolex.

On an adjoining page, whiskey is advertised. Whiskey will either help or hinder your game in many ways, depending on your point of view. To calm your jitters before the opening tee there is "Glenmorangie, single malt scotch whiskey." This whiskey is "unnecessarily well made." It must be, due to the fact that the bottle in the ad is as tall as the Championship Trophy Claret Jug standing next to it. The scotch apparently is a major sponsor of "The Open, at Royal Liverpool, 2014," an original from Scotland. The label shows the scotch as ten years old, unfortunately a mere 140 years younger than the Claret Jug itself.

Page ten advertises "Bubba Watson-Oakley Golf Apparel." The "unorthodox, untamed and unimaginable are not qualities of a professional golfer, unless you're Bubba." This is also an accurate account of my neighbor, Dizzy Bob, who is very unorthodox and untamed. Bob has a hitting net in his backyard, and beyond the net is an open area that gives way to a marshy, gray, mucky creek. A third of his practice balls find their way over or around the net and into the protected wetlands. His swing is so quirky that it looks like he is trying to stab a slithering snake that has appeared between his too-narrow of a stance. The Oakley ad boldly states "disruptive by design," unlike neighbor Bob, who is disruptive by practice. One thing I've learned from this page is that we now know that the "O" represents the brand "Oakley" on Bubba's shirt, front and back. I always thought it odd that good ol' General Lee driving southern boy was an alum of Oregon University, which we now learn he is not.

Another page features prescription golf glasses: "SportRx, specialized golf lenses for all prescriptions" with "light adjusting lenses, digital lens technology, contrast enhancing features, and depth perception improvement." They could've said, "They look cool on your face," and that would've done it for most of us. Or, "You can wear these after drinking a pint of the Scotch whiskey featured on the previous pages and still look cool." However, I'm dubious about these. The guy in the picture is standing on a beach, rippling ocean waves behind him and making a bad swing with the club. If he's wearing these specialized lenses featuring the newest technology, then how did he end up inside a lateral hazard on the beach? And there is no one else in sight to boot. Once, I was handed a pair of sunglasses to test and later report on them. Testing new equipment and accessories was a benefit of becoming a lifetime member of the PGA Tour Partners Club. These sunglasses were made to enhance your ability to read the green better. With these, I was informed you can see, "Every blade of grass and every contour more clearly." That was true enough, I noticed after wearing them for two rounds, and as a bonus, they allowed me to see my ball skip by the hole with a visual acuity I had never experienced before.

"You CAN shoot lower scores!" the next advertisement shouts at the reader, in large thirty-two point font. This is the "Dave Pelz Scoring Game School." I like the sound of that. Mr. Pelz has locations in five states and in England and Ireland too. Log on to "pelzgolf.com" to enroll and learn "Dave's latest tips." Finally, real golf tips from a real teaching pro and without a catch. Interestingly, one of his locations is a golf club in New York City. Where did they fit it in a city of eight million people, and will I have to take a taxi to get there?

Me: "Please take me to Centennial Golf Club."

Rahimi, the driver: "No golf club here. This is New York City. City of eight million people. No golf club."

"What about the one in Central Park?"

"Aaah yes, Central Park. I take you there. Do you have time for tee?"

"No, it's for instruction only."

"My cousin, Ramel, he is good golf guy, he can give you lesson."

"No thanks, I have a date with Mr. Pelz."

"Oh, you date the men? Very interesting."

"Never mind, just dump me in the middle of the park, and I'll find my own way to Centennial Golf Club."

No secrets to shooting birdies in the magazine yet. You can, though, have "accuracy you can trust." Digging deeper and reading (glancing) further into the glossy mag's pages, I notice the "SkyCaddie Linx" that gives "dynamic green distances from your angle of approach, with exact green shapes and up to 40 targets per hole." Although the item that looks like a wristwatch seems like a nice accessory that you can personalize and match to the colors of your wardrobe, it looks like cheating to me. By contrast, there is no cost to stepping off the distances based on sprinkler head numbers and estimating the yardage on your own. If the angle of your approach is so far off the fairway, you won't see the green anyway, and at that moment won't care about its shape. Just hit it to the center of the green, according to Jack Nicklaus.

"More spin, more types of shot, more ways to shoot lower scores." You just gotta get the new "Vokey Spin Milled 5 Wedges" from Titleist. These assuredly are upgrades from my "Whack 'em to the Green" wedges I've had for years. These new wedges "provide players with a distinct performance advantage. They deliver maximum spin thanks to new deeper TX3™ grooves that channel away grass and sand for improved contact between the ball and groove edge." And to think that all these years I've been swiping the clubface clean with a plain old kitchen towel borrowed from my wife. Now the wedges will do that for me. On top of that, the professional analysts on golf telecasts tell us that when grass gets between the clubface and the ball, the ball always flies further than when it's free of grass. There is scientific proof of that. If golfers want more distance, as most do, then it makes sense to manufacture clubs with grass already embedded into the clubface. Club makers can make milled wedges, so why not milled drivers? And, better yet, why not drivers with grass permanently stuck on the face for more distance off the tee?

Artificial grass is available, or they can come to my neighbor's house and dig up his front yard, since his grass stays green all year long. The Titleist ad continues, "Get serious about lowering your scores." We the golfers are serious, but what about you, Titleist people? If you were more serious, you would manufacture clubs with grass already on the clubface for "improved performance."

Having gotten through twenty-four pages of the magazine at this point, I notice the game improvement ads start shifting from wedges to putters. "Odyssey" claims to be the #1 putter in golf. Under total disclosure, I own and use an "Odyssey" putter, and have for many years used the same one. But this one is elevated as "the new Tank 2-Ball."

"A heavier head, shaft, and counter balance weight produce a Tour-preferred balance point for higher MOI and greater stability." This one may be suitable for my neighbor, Dizzy Bob, but not for me, I can assure you. And for one simplified reason—any club or accessory with the word "tank" in it does not connote a comfortable condition. There's enough potential for trouble on the course, and I can't think of why anyone would want to "tank a putt."

Dizzy Bob could use more stability on the course. We once played a round on a typical early summer's day and by the second hole he was walking in circles. In the cart heading to the tee, he drove erratically as if he had just come out of Murphy's Bar and Grille from the night before. His face was egg white—all of his natural coloring had vanished. A few of us thought he was having a heart attack or stroke; we knew Bob didn't drink alcohol, so the Murphy's Bar wasn't the reason. He assured us he was not having life-threatening problems, claiming he had chronic bronchial congestion that had to be kept in check on a daily basis. According to his self-diagnosis, he was suffering from a bout of vertigo because he failed to apply Vicks VapoRub that day.

Bob has only one lung, and the smelly miracle ointment helps him to breathe through his nose and mouth, opening up his airways. If his airways aren't clear enough, then his ears get clogged up, which, in turn, causes vertigo. Looking down at the golf ball with vertigo makes the entire fairway spin like a kids' toy top. As he tried to hit the ball, he looked like he was trying to screw his six-foot-five body into the ground starting with his spikes, twisting his torso like an intertwined pretzel while missing the ball wildly.

Vicks VapoRub should advertise in the golf magazines as "a savior for those with vertigo." Although the ad would be just as effective if it read, "Need help seeing the ball, even if you don't have vertigo? Try Vicks VapoRub!" Golfers will try anything.

Still undeterred, I'm now even more interested in becoming a "birdie machine," so I continue reading. One ad shows a smiling middle-aged man with gleaming white teeth, a stubble beard, beginner mustache, and gray speckled hair. He appears to be glancing over his left shoulder. The enlarged caption reads, "Bend the rules." Thinking this is about the golden rules of golf, I am definitely intrigued, only to discover he is selling or attempting to sell flexible eyeglasses—"memory metal titanium eyewear that always returns to its original shape." This titanium compound metal seems to be a miracle metal, as it is used in every piece of golfing equipment these days. The male model in this ad is everywhere, too. Turn a coupla' pages and he pronounces, "Welcome to our world." Looks like the same man, only this time he has a serious look, no smile, and is peering straight at the reader. This guy means business, sitting in the cockpit of his shiny lemon yellow single-engine speed plane topping off at 500 mph, the page tells us.

On the right side of the full page ad is a terrific looking silver metallic Breitling watch. No doubt made of titanium, it is described as a "Chronomat 44 Flying Fish." The Flying Fish describes either the airplane or the watch; I'm not certain which. The fine print reveals that "it is for these elite aviators that Breitling develops its chronographs: sturdy, functional and ultra-high performance instruments all equipped with movements chronometer-certified by the COSC." There are plenty of other dials, gages, and instruments on this precision piece, so it is more than just a watch and can do more than tell time, unlike my twenty-two dollar Timex. But can it make me a birdie machine?

Convinced now that I must be in the market for a dozen Titleist golf balls, another eye-catching ad appears for Callaway, a stiff Titleist competitor. "The world's first tour balls designed to fly farther with HEX aerodynamics customized for different swing speeds." There are three different balls to choose from in this category, each one appearing in the ad like the planet of faraway Saturn with its atmospheric equator rings. Since average golfers hit the ball around 210 yards from the tee, these dimpled spheres must have titanium in their core to make it into outer space.

There are more balls to get excited about in the upcoming pages. Nike has the "RZN" ball which is "longer, faster, and more stable thanks to a game-changing technology we call the Speedlock RZN core." Could this RZN core be titanium, the metal named after a mythical creature of strength? More turned pages and more golf balls on sale. Srixon quotes pro golfer Keegan Bradley in its ad: "Better isn't about clinging to the past. It's not about pretending to be the future. If you are crazy enough to question good enough, you might just get better." His quotation is very Yoda-esque. Keegan doesn't look too happy here, much like Yoda from *Star Wars*. His head is tilted downward, his eyes are squinting, and there's a sadness to his frown that conveys a desire to clobber the beejeebus out of the Srixon ball.

No wonder Keegan Bradley appears angry. On the very next page there he is standing in the middle of a rental car parking lot with hands on hips, glaring out over the edges of the garage. He seems perplexed as to which car he should choose, or else his caddy/driver failed to meet him with his rented car. With a full bag of clubs at his side, standing there all alone in his golfing attire with his caddy nowhere in sight, Keegan, a high energy on-the-go guy, looks ready to knock the stuffing out of a few golf balls once he finally reaches the driving range.

The single best personal improvement item in golf over the past five years has to be the men and women's microfiber moisture-wicking shirts. Can't argue with the truth here. Nowadays there's no reason to come home with a dripping wet, one hundred percent cotton polo shirt weighing twenty pounds more than when you started your round on a hot, humid day in the south, or north for that matter, too. You probably didn't play any better in the microfiber shirt than in the old-fashioned polo, but you feel like you did, and that's what matters most. The feel.

According to another manufacturer, Adidas, the "climalite shirt, Permanence seco, permanece c`omodo! Con Climalite permaneces seco porque absorbe todo el sudor de tu piel." Oh shucks, they wrote it in Spanish, and there seems to be a grande amount of "permanence" in the description. According to my translator, Señor Arribe it says, "Stay dry, stay comfortable. Climalite keeps your body dry by drawing sweat away from the skin." I heard there is fabric in shorts that contain moisture-wicking properties, too. Be cautious here, folks—too much improvement in your yardage and game all at once could really upset your old golf buddies. You might be out there in your latest, coolest fabric all alone, in ninety-five degree heat and humidity, with your cotton-heavy friends in the air-conditioned clubhouse drinking cold ones to replenish their fluid intake.

At last! I have found the "secret to becoming a birdie machine." Buried 108 pages into the magazine is pro golfer Justin Rose. Fifteen different angles of his fluid golf swing are depicted, although they're not exactly fluid because the images are standard still pictures. There are four lessons outlined on four separate pages, which are mostly covered with pictures of Rose. Reading intently, I learn about the new rules I should follow: 1. "New Rules for Hitting Fairways." 2. "New Rules for Hitting Greens." 3. "New Rules for Wedging it Close," and 4. "New Rules for Sinking Putts." After just reading these headlines, I realize I'm already in trouble of not becoming a birdie machine. New rules should be followed, and I'm still stuck learning the old ones. I tell myself it's good advice to heed the four lessons on these pages and put them at the top of my

New Year's resolutions, followed by my continuation of my "no chit-chat policy" on the course.

According to the article, Justin has made 3025 birdies during his PGA Tour career. He carded 384 birdies in 2006, his best birdie year, and in his U.S. Open winning performance of 2013, he had fifteen birdies in his four rounds. I had fifteen birdies all year. Justin Rose is my new hero, and I believe his secret lies in his red golf shirt, not with his syrupy sweet perfect swing. In each photograph he is wearing his red stay-dry shirt. If you have ever seen Tiger Woods play during tournaments, you'd know that he also wears a red stay-cool shirt on Sundays, and he's another birdie machine. I only own one red golf shirt, so I'm headed to the nearest clothing outlet for a dozen more red ones. At least I will *look* like a birdie machine, even if I don't play like one.

There is one item that hasn't seen many changes over the course of the past one hundred years, an item we all desperately need, the little golf pencil. The only added feature to the six-sided lead pencil is the eraser, which adds a quarter of an inch to the overall length of the three and a half inch original. The girth is always the same in order to fit into the pencil attachment of the cart. The golf cart manufacturers have improved on their ergonomic, aerodynamic designs each year, all centered around the little pencil holder attached to the steering wheel. Pencil makers caved in to the demands of players all over the world to "add an eraser, or else!" By "or else" they meant they'd start using ink pens instead, since the scorekeepers couldn't erase their markings on the card anyway. When the Scripto and Bic pen producers began working on a smaller three and a half-inch version to fit in the cart, the pencil makers wised up and added erasers, to the delight of golfers everywhere.

The golf cart itself has seen several improvements over the years, but there remains one more that has been overlooked. The cart manufactures must put an end to that annoying, high-pitched whining sound the cart makes when it is put in reverse. *BeeeeeeeeWeeeeWeee* is a horrible sound. I suggest a more pleasant sound to replace this deafening and crude nuisance on the level of a garbage truck going backwards. We are aware that the OSHA people who make the rules want us to be safe and forewarn our playing competitors before we run over them and squash them up like an unwanted kitchen cockroach. My replacement would be a soft, sexy voice to announce the backup warning. And the voice can be customized depending upon the sex of the driver who initiates the cart movement. For men drivers, a Marilyn Monroe voiceover that says something like, "Hey big boy, move away, I'm about to move my booty in your direction." Followed by a short giggle. For women drivers, a manly voice sounding like Arnold Swartzenager: "I'm coming back, move it or I will terminate you." It could even be more ethnic, such as Rev. Martin Luther King, Jr: "I have a dream, that if you don't get out of the way, you will be overcome." Perhaps a bit more edgy such as comedian Chris Rock: "Get the F*k out of my way, I'll kick your ass, M*F*er." Or from Slyvester Stalone: "Yo, Adrian, I'll punch your lights out if'n you don't move outta da' way." There'd be one for the gay and lesbian community, too: "I don't mean to bother you, but I'm backing up here, and we have rights."

Another option could be soft, gentle music. For Italians, the theme from "The Godfather," for Irish, "Danny Boy," bagpipes for the Scots, and for old-timers, the senior citizens, a song from Frank Sinatra: "Start spreading the news, I'm backing up, cause I'm doing it my way." Finally, for the younger generation, a Rap verse from 50 Cent or LL Cool J.: "Back it up, back it up, pump it up, pump it up."

All of these options will be offered on the dashboard, it is up to the driver which one he chooses.

Other cart improvements are on the horizon, according to the entrepreneurs represented at the annual golf showcase from Orlando, Florida each January. One such innovation is the "Golf Board." This design is a skateboard with a place for one bag of clubs on the back. The only power comes from the golfer himself who pushes along with one foot until there is enough energy for the board to roll along on its' own. This will work, I suppose, if the course you are playing is all downhill. Somewhat dangerous, even a fourteen-year-old teenager might crash into unmovable objects. Much was the case of this young daredevil who was skate boarding on the hills and curves of the Kiln Creek golf course in Newport News, Virginia recently. Having a fiberglass board with intricate designs of a human skull with greenish snakes protruding from its blood red eyes, he nearly ran into our cart as we ascended from one of the tunnels from a road underpass. Although he missed the cart, he crashed face first into the concrete wall encompassing the circular tunnel. No helmet, no elbow or knee pads on this kid, but he did survive with a broad smile and a fist pump, saying out loud, "Yeah, I almost made the corner this time!" Farther down the course, we spotted him again tumbling down a 60-degree paved slope and into some boulders at the bottom. "This one is great, at the end there is soft grass to land on," again smiling as if he was getting paid to do these "tricks."

Another newer design is the "Golf Skate Caddy." This one has a small battery pack that powers the GPS, the rangefinder, lights, and horn. It has an accessory port for charging up your smartphones and similar devices. You're going to need the horn because this one quickly weaves in and around obstacles like a surfer on a twenty-foot wave, avoiding other surfboarders. There is a place for your clubs, of course, but no way to hold on. Guys with poor balance, like Dizzy Bob, need a guide bar to hang onto or else they become Evil Knievel trying to hurdle over fairway bunkers. Without brakes to stop either the Golf Board, or the Golf Skate Caddy you'll have to run into the short wooden poles that mark the fairways or the out of bounds markers, I'm guessing.

The "Golf Bike" seems reasonable, though. It allows exercise while peddling and functionality while carrying a set of clubs. And it has useable brakes, a desired benefit. I hope it has a cup holder or can holder for the beer or iced tea, otherwise you'd be like a juggling clown sitting atop his unicycle trying to steer, drink your beverage and holding on simultaneously.

I receive dozens of email solicitations every day regarding golf magazines, golf instruction, and golf-related stories. One recently caught my attention, as it was a clever advertisement. A new putter called the "Z-Ball Putter" had hit the market. The marketers introduced this eye-catching product with the slogan "See Z-ball, putt Z-ball." The ad reads, "This new putter has a deadly French connection. When you brag about your KICK X -Z-Ball putter after sinking putt after big money putt, you'll kick up your heels and shout: 'See Z ball! Putt Z ball! Hole Z ball!'" Sacrebleu, mon ami, no one would—or should—shout that out. Your golf buddies will be calling "Z psychiatrist" on your behalf if you utter those words.

The ad continues: "It's easy to aim, Zebra style lines with a contrasting ball shape improve putter alignment at address and throughout the stroke. Plus the black satin PVD finish reduces glare and accentuates alignment lines. In other words, you know exactly where the ball's going." It all sounds pretty enticing to me, but usually the slope, angle, and speed of the green will determine where the ball is going. You will know roughly about where the ball is headed, but *exactly* where is anybody's guess.

Complementing the "Z-Ball Putter" is a remarkable new ball marker offered by Iron-lad Golf (www.Iron-ladgolf.com), which "helps you read the green better," claims the ad. This marker aids in reading the slope, grain, and speed of the greens. You can even see the Levelhead in action on their video. "Place the Levelhead directly behind your ball. Depending on the lie of your ball, the bubble in the Levelhead will tilt left, right, up, or down. When it's sitting left or right, hit the ball in that direction to catch the break. If the bubble is pointing up, you need to hit it harder, pointing down, slower." The ad also instructs you to "Place it. Get your read. Putt. Sink. It couldn't be any more easy, right?" Not exactly. Many putting surfaces are contoured in different ways, the dreaded "double breaker" for example. The Levelhead reads the first break, but doesn't account for the next break. The new technology costs only $29.99, shipped in a special felt-covered pouch. You can get your Levelhead marker in a color choice of blue, black, or red. It looks like a miniature alien spaceship, the kind that once flew over Roswell, New Mexico. Interestingly, it is not offered in green.

Easier than using that marker (and a video is not necessary to explain) is the original way to mark a ball by placing a coin behind it when you pick it up. Either a penny or dime will do. As this method costs just a penny or dime, it won't break the bank. Even if you forget to pick up your penny, or if your playing partner puts it in his pocket, you'll need to lose 2,999 of them to equal the cost of one Levelhead. Maybe the Levelhead is worth a try; at least it comes in various colors. The blasé penny only comes in a dirty copper color, which is a huge disadvantage unless you're colorblind like my pal "Jaybird." He sees everything in black, white, and gray.

As you pace around trying to judge the angle of the green, you should have the most comfortable and stable golf shoes on the market. The Ecco high performance shoe has gotten even better than last year's model. At least that's what the email says in bold print, so naturally I have to read on. As the ad introduces me to the "BIOM Hybrid 2," I realize I musta' missed the "Hybrid 1." This shoe is incredible:"Hydromax, highly water repellant, durable, and breathable" with "direct-injected PU." My shoes already have enough "pee-yew," so I don't think this is a desirable selling point. The ad highlights their "high tech, one piece construction without the use of glue or stitching" and includes arrows directing the reader to the heel of the shoe. "Natural motion." But what if the wear-er exhibits an unnatural motion by walking in a "clip-clop" stomping pattern like my friend "Moose" Spencer. Moose, at six-feet four-inches and proportionately built, including size fourteen sidewalk destroyers, sometimes forgets to replace the flagstick and marches off to his cart with putter in one hand and pole in the other. He seems to be a one-man color guard leading a Fourth of July parade until he realizes his wrongdoing. The shoe with "Dual density design"—sounds impressive, as do "E-DTS" and the claim that they are "constructed from wear resistant material." Wonder what that material could be? I hope it is not the same titanium material that causes sparks to fly when hitting a rock in laboratory tests. Your feet will not only have the "pee-yew factor" but will also keep you warm in the winter when the sparks fly as you walk over rocks and the paved cart path.

Thinking that this shoe looks comfortable and inviting, I'd suggest Jaybird to buy a pair. He won't care about the colors, either, since they are offered in plain white, brown and black. All the same to him. They are all "bee-u-timus," a word he invented.

There is another shoe that offers stability recently on the market as shown in an Internet ad. This is the "Nike Lunar Control 3." The ad says simply, "There's always better." I'd be bit more interested if it stated, "There's always better than most," one of my favorite expressions. This shoe looks sleek, modern, and hip. These must have been inspired by Astronaut Buzz Aldrin, who was the second space explorer who walked on the moon. It has never been a proven fact that these men actually walked on moon's surface. It was difficult to make out exactly where they were due to the grainy black and white pictures shown on our nineteen-inch television screens of the "moon landing." Who exactly was holding the camera lens when all this was unfolding? The video pictures of the Sixties and Seventies reveal only the heavily suited astronaut and the rugged rocky dust covered ground below his lunar boots. Now, forty years hence, Nike has their newest design, of the Lunar golf shoe. This is either a coincidence or a clear connection with a regional Nike headquarters location in rural Nevada.

Another e-mail headline appealing to every weekend golfer reads, "Fixing Your Slice is a Waste of Time!" I've been saying that for years, for righties simply aim more to the left and don't worry about slicing. The ad tempts the reader with "a free video that reveals one weird swing trick that adds ups to twenty accurate yards to your drives." The swings of slicers are already weird, or else the ball wouldn't spin waywardly to the right each time. It's easy to skip this video.

All of these magazine and TV ads, e-mails, videos, and info mercials claim to improve golfers' equipment and, ultimately, their skills. Technology for game improvement has come a long way in the past several years, and instruction via the Internet, YouTube, and DVD videos can certainly help. I wholeheartedly enjoy reading the instruction tips in all the golfing magazines, as well as the advertisements sent to me in various forms. I haven't meant to disparage any new gadget, gizmo, or enhancement promoted by the professionals "as seen on TV." But if anyone is truly interested in having a better golf game and better results, then this one tip has always been the best tip: Practice, practice, practice, preferably with a PGA pro at the nearest golf course.

CHAPTER 10

Hank-Enstein and the Dark Side

WALKING DOWN THE ninth fairway, Hank turned to Tom and me and remarked, "I'm not playing well today because my socks are too heavy." Socks too heavy? Really? All the years I've played this game I don't ever remember anyone using that excuse for poor play. I've heard excuses such as socks that were too tight or didn't fit well, or even socks with holes in the soles that could affect one's comfort level. But, never too heavy.

It's a shame there wasn't the "Ultimate Golf Sock" on the market back then. This sock, of ankle height and plushness beyond compare, is currently offered to the modern golf junkie. The ads describe them as the best socks ever. But how does anyone know if they are the best ever? We all should own a pair; golf scores would be lower throughout the country. With their patented airflow technology, they're cooler and more comfortable than run-of-the-mill socks. At last, I can throw away my calf-high tube socks. But how much air can enter through one's shoes to the socks, making contact against the skin of one's actual feet? The sock scientists have this calculated as air pressure per square foot. Airflow technology sounds terrific. Hank could've used that. The socks come with moisture management for no extra charge. With descriptions much like those seen in car ads on TV and in magazines, these comfort machines have cushioned soles—"Y-shaped" heels that won't slip. Hank could've used that too. They have no-slip tops and smooth toe seams according to the advertisement. The only thing missing is the "fine Corinthian leather" and token spokesperson—preferably Carl Montalban with his Andalusian accent.

Hank, middle-aged with a slender physique, once wore a bucket hat with an automatic fan circulating inside to help cool the top of his head as he walked. At the front of the hat was a small flap that allowed air in as he walked, which in turn activated the tiny fan inside. The motion of the fan was dictated by how fast the wearer walked, but it was more novelty than useful because his head sweated as much as anyone else's, as far as I could determine. And the fan made the hat a bit too heavy and lopsided as he looked down while swinging his Paul Bunyon-esque chop. It jolted to the right side of his forehead, obstructing his view of the ground below.

Hank Swanson was a respected officer with the Army Reserves and on active duty for many years as the Training Officer for an entire battalion of Reservists. He was in an important leadership and supervisory position in the military. Unfortunately, he played golf like a new Infantry recruit learning to dig a foxhole removing globs of turf with every swing.

Off the course he was serious, professionally dedicated, well-educated as a Michigan State alum, soft spoken and engaging. On the course his moody personality was revealed like a crazed monster, a "Hank-Enstein." He didn't just throw clubs—he threw bags, balls, tees, towels, and gloves. Pro golfer, hot-tempered club thrower Tommy Bolt could learn a few things from him. Hank-Enstein may have inspired a startup industry associated with bad behavior. According to BogeyPro.com a complete series of lessons have been created for the ideal club and bag thrower.

"There is no better way to honor another triple digit round than the 'ol bag toss," the lesson's introduction explains. "The granddaddy of golf showmanship, it requires a bit of panache, a strong back, and knowledge of elementary physics. For cleaner clubs, execute from the edge of the nearest pond." The accompanying illustrations show a Hank-Enstein cloned character tossing his bag. Figure "A" shows how to begin with bent knees, locked elbow, and a low center of gravity. Figure "B" completes the toss with a full shoulder turn, finishes with high leg kick, high trajectory with hips rotated toward the target, and a full transfer of weight to the front leg."

Hank's tirades occurred at least a few times per round. Before leaving the first tee, Tom and I covertly placed a side bet choosing when and at what hole the first explosion would happen. Tom, a *Golfstradamus*, had a flair for predicting upcoming situations and usually won those bets, since he had known Hank longer than I had and could read his moods more easily.

It's a shame that modern technology hadn't been perfected the year we went on a buddies' trip to Myrtle Beach. Hank could've used a smartphone app to access real-time traffic, road maps, parking areas, and weather reports while on the road. Not just for the 350-mile trip to Myrtle Beach from

Virginia but for navigating to and around the golf courses. Arriving at one of the courses, Hank maneuvered his mini-van down the cart path leading past the bag drop area and onward to the first fairway. The GPS navigator would have sternly warned him to "turn right, make a U-turn," adding "re-calculating, you numbskull" with that edgy attitude of hers.

Tom Rogers, longtime friend and avid golfer, introduced me to Hank one Saturday morning. Tom, a friendly and gentle man, was well regarded by all who knew him. He was a govern-ment employee supervisor in Human Resources and a gradu-ate of Virginia Tech. He performed in the local community Lion's Club Variety Show held annually in February for chari-table purposes. It was an amateurish, yet entertaining, show held in one of the nearby high school auditoriums. Lots of singing, most of it done by rising entertainers aspiring to make it big, and plenty of laughs too. Tom was one of the "four stars" of comedy, the "EndMen" who appeared at the corners of the stage to put on their skits and tell jokes in between the acts. Tom used several of our golf jokes during the show, material derived from conversations we'd overheard or been a part of during our days on the course. With a stage name of "Monroe" (pronounced "Muun-roe" in a distinctive southern drawl) Tom expertly delivered his punch lines, receiving the approval of laughter from the audience.

Muun-roe: "A detective walks into a golfer's house where a murder has been committed."

Theopolis, the other "Endman": "What did he say?"

Muun-roe: "Sir, did you kill this intruder?"

Theopolis: "Then what was the reply?"

Muun-roe: "Yes, detective, I did."

Seeing the bloody 3-iron lying next to the victim, the detective asked: "Did you hit him with this club?"

"Yes, sir, I did."

Theopolis: "How many times did you hit him?"

Muun-roe: "It was six, seven, or eight times—so, just put me down for a five."

After months of playing weekend golf together, Monroe, Hank, and I decided it was time to take a buddies' trip to Myrtle Beach for a week-long indulgence on the grandstand. Scotty Dez, our active duty Air Force companion joined us for those five much-anticipated days of serenity and gluttonous golf. Arriving to our destination late in the afternoon, we took on one of those lighted par-3 courses. It would turn out to be the last enjoyable round on the trip for Hank.

The next morning, the weather wasn't cooperating. The drizzly rain and chilly wind weren't surprising, given that it was mid-April. It was the kind of day that if you were home and looked out your front window, you would not head to the golf course at 7 a.m. But because we were at the golf capital of the east coast, we were there to play. Besides, the weather was promising, with sunshine forecasted for later that day. At least that's what we believed. Unfortunately Hank's mood changed faster than a rodeo clown's face being gored by a charging bull. He dropped us off near the bag drop and sped off in his van, declaring the day unfit for outdoor activity. We played on, but the question remained in our minds—"Will he return to pick us up?"

The next morning, the brighter, warmer Carolina day imparted a feeling of freshness and newness to the air. Birds chirped everywhere as the aroma of pink and purplish azaleas and yellow jasmine filled our noses. The dogwood trees were in full bloom, and the scent of pine awaited us. But even this picturesque day couldn't shake Hank from his dark moody doldrums. Instead of golfing with us, he drove off to the Waccamaw Pottery Shopping Outlet for a fun-filled day of indoor shopping. The entire week progressed in this same manner. Hank-Enstein's weeklong golf trip resulted in a drive of over seven hundred round-trip miles to play one round of par-3 golf. The rest of his time was spent hanging out in a condo-hotel and shopping at an outlet mall.

Three years later I was invited to join a group of twenty guys on another buddies' trip to Myrtle. Scotty Dez arranged this trip with many of his coworkers attending. He also arranged the hotel room assignments, and because I didn't know these guys well, he assigned me to share a room with Ron Krueger. After one night with him, I'd rather it would've been Freddy Krueger from the horror movie.

I had to leave before sunrise for the seven-hour drive to Myrtle Beach in order to meet the groups' first afternoon tee time at one o'clock. It was a pleasant enough mid-April day, plenty of azure blue skies with mild temperatures. Yet the ordeal was exhausting after the drive, followed by four and one half hours of golf. It was about to get worse.

I met Ron Kreuger for the very first time at hotel check-in where the entire group had rendezvoused after an evening meal following golf. A man in his early fifties, he was a ruffian and quite boorish. If he hadn't told me otherwise, I imagined he was raised in a cave with wild animals. As we unpacked our suitcases, and waited for nightfall, he painstakingly revealed his life's experiences providing each meticulous detail.

"I grew up near where you live now," Ron informed me. "But now the place has changed, and I haven't been back since."

"How long did you live there?" I made the fatal mistake of extending the conversation.

"Well, let's see, Mom and Pappy (yes he said "Pappy"), owned a liquor store for fifteen years when I was young, so it musta' been that long. After school, I would stop at the store to tell 'em I was going home. I spent a lot of time at the store."

"Hey, do you want a shot of scotch?" his speech slurred from an afternoon diet of whiskey on the course.

"No, Ron, I'm headed to bed after a long day, thanks anyway."

As I lay there waiting for sleep to arrive, he rambled on for another hour or more. Being sleep-deprived and half-awake, it wasn't clear how long he continued woolgathering. "… An only child, not married, never married but wanted to be, twelve years in the Army, received disability from shrapnel from a hand grenade explosion in Vietnam, moved to Richmond, Virginia, and now works for the Department of Defense, whereby he knows the others on this trip…"

"It was probably one of your squad members who threw the grenade," I muttered in my somnolent state.

"Quite possibly," he retorted, as we both managed a subdued laughter.

Minutes later I heard the door slam and then it became a perfectly silent room. Aaah, finally some sleep.

At 1:17 am, I sensed an intruder stumbling around the darkened hotel room. As I peered with eyes halfway open, I detected a shadowy figure near me and could hear his deep breathing with grunting like a large dog when you get near his bone he's chewing on.

Ron had returned after closing down the hotel's lounge and bar with a few other tortured souls. This mad dog came back and was off the chain.

Not yet wanting to be fully awake, I ignored the sounds, until his two hundred twenty pound, five-foot ten-inch blubberish body sat on the edge of my bed.

"Ron, this ain't your bed, I'm trying to sleep over here," I blurted out.

"Oh, sorry, at least I'm in the right room," he cackled mixed with un-auditory sounds.

The night continued with grunts, groans, and snoring which could have been mistaken for the rumble of the roof of a house being torn off by virtue of a class 5 tornado. The 7 a.m. alarm couldn't come soon enough.

At the breakfast buffet where the group assembled before the days' worth of golf, with bleary red-veined eyes, I caught the attention of Scotty Dez.

"Scotty, you have connected me with a freakish monster," as I recounted the beastly tales of the worst night of my sleepless night. "Why did you assign me to room with this fiend?"

I gruffly inquired.

"No one else dared to be with him," he replied. "Since you are friendly and don't know him, you were the best person to double with."

"You mean the *only* person."

I wasn't finished dealing with Ron Kreuger that day. Scotty had made the pairings of foursomes in advance and Ron was part of my group. Before arriving at the first tee, he started out with two Bloody Mary's. By the end of the second hole, he was offering three of us to guzzle from his bottle of whiskey. I am not a teetotaler, occasionally enjoy some adult beverage, but it wasn't quite 9 a.m., so his offer was ignored by all three of us.

"Oh hell, it's five o'clock somewhere," Ron shouted out for the benefit of all golfers on the front nine. His voice got louder with each ensuing gulp of alcohol. Admittedly not much of a golfer, he blabbered nonstop throughout the round, only pausing frequently to take another mouthful of whiskey. I doubt that a comprehensive course in golf etiquette or human behavior could ever cure him as he disrupted everyone's backswings with his chatter.

"Does anyone know why there are eighteen holes on a golf course?" he clamored to the three of us standing on the tee box. When no one answered in order to avoid his shenanigans, he continued, "At the dawn of golf, the Scots drank a shot of their whiskey after every hole, and when their bottle was emptied, the game was over. It lasted eighteen holes. Well, I'm here to prove 'em wrong. My Scotch is empty after fourteen holes," he stammered.

Following that afternoons' unbearable scene, Ron and I parted company. Thoughtfully, Scotty found a separate room for him. It was either that or Ron would have to sleep out on the balcony of our hotel room for the remainder of the week. The next morning, after a restful night, I awoke to a slip of paper discreetly slipped under the door leading to my room:

"May the spirit of Ron Krueger haunt you for the rest of your days."

We didn't have to travel as far to meet another character from the "dark side," a total stranger. Like Hank-Enstein, Stevie Logan seemed nice enough, a likeable creature. The starter matched us up with him at Riverfront Golf Course in Suffolk, Virginia. Riverfront, a pleasant yet demanding track, welcomes golfers of all ability levels. Stevie believed he was in the professional category, judging by his superior attitude and the way he walked. I think you can discover a lot about a person by observing the way he walks. Sorta like "beauty is in the eye of the beholder" explanation, you can judge a personality by the manner in which he or she walks. To my amazement, there have been studies regarding this theory. One study by Cindi May, Professor of Psychology at the College of Charleston is titled: *What Does the Way You Walk Say About You? Psychologists explore the outer limits of first impressions.*

"First impressions are powerful and are formed in all sorts of social settings, from job interviews and first dates to court rooms and classrooms. We regularly make snap judgments about others, deciding whether people are trustworthy, confident, extraverted, likable, and more. Although we have all heard the old adage, "Don't judge a book by its cover," we do just that. And at the same time that we are judging others, we, in turn, communicate a great deal of information about ourselves—often unwittingly—that others use to size us up. John Thoresen, Quoc Vuong, and Anthony Atkinson addressed this question in a series of experiments where participants judged personality traits on the basis of body movements alone. The scientists first videotaped male and female volunteers as they walked roughly twenty-five feet. From these videos, they created stick-figure depictions of each walker, eliminating all information about age, attractiveness, weight, clothing, race, and gender. The only information available to observers was the gait of the walker, conveyed in the form of a two-dimensional stick figure. Participants in these studies rated each stick figure walker on six trait scales: adventurousness, extraversion, neuroticism, trustworthiness, warmth, and approachability."

In other research, experts reveal what your walk says about you. Talk is often cheap, but the way you walk can speak volumes about you, according to body language experts Patti Wood, author of *Snap: Making the Most of First Impressions*, and Eliot Hoppe, communication trainer and author. Although cultural and environmental factors can weigh in, they believe a person's body language can reflect mood, emotions, and even personality.

"Body language conveys the true emotion of how you feel," Hoppe says. "And a lot of these movements are unconscious. We're absolutely unaware that we're doing body language can reflect a person's character, Wood has found in her research. She believes different walks can fit into the DISC personality profile: Drivers (who display dominance) walk quickly with intent and don't like to stop once they know where they're

headed; influencers often act emotionally, changing direction often; supporters who show steadiness walk politely with
their arms close to their bodies and might stop to speak with
others; cautious people, who Wood calls "correctors," walk
precisely and follow foot <u>traffic rules</u>.

Stevie attempted to size up our golfing expertise even before
we arrived at the first tee. His hesitation to join us was evi-
dent. Crazy—who wouldn't want to be associated with Tom
"Muunroe" Rogers and myself? Not wanting to get paired up
with hackers or beginners, he asked about our golf handicaps.
"Good enough," said Muunroe. "You'll see," I remarked, adding to the intrigue of gamesmanship.

We didn't ask him about his handicap, mostly because we
didn't care. We play with golfers of all abilities; having fun is
our measure of a good day.

Stevie striped the first drive and Muunroe followed with a
good one, yet mine tailed right, a mini-slice that was shorter
than the others. My second shot fell short of the par-4 green,
while Muunroe was closer and Stevie hit the center of the
green. As he sped forward he looked back over his shoulder,
probably thinking about abandoning our threesome. Stevie
made his 2–putt par, Muunroe chipped and 2–putted for his
routine bogey, and my chip landed three feet from the cup
for an easy tap-in par. After four holes of matching pars and
bogeys, Stevie realized that pars could be gotten in several
ways. His attitude and demeanor abruptly changed to Mister
Nice Guy, now I will talk to you. We passed his golfing test;
we were "play-aahs."

The game continued for the next two and a half hours, with
Stevie even drinking a few of the beers we purchased and had

on ice. Our strokes were roughly equivalent and pars were generally made, with some bogeys and birdies mixed in for equal measure. We "Three Amigos" yukked it up.

The rule of the day was "cart path only" due to the soaking rains the night before. The fairways were squishy under our shoes, yet playable, and in half the locations the ground was completely dry. When playing "cart path only," the law of physics demands that your golf ball be hit to the opposite edge of the fairway from the cart path. Therefore, a mega-amount of walking is involved. After trudging over fairways for thirteen holes and consuming many Bud Lights, Muunroe decided to abandon the rule on the fourteenth hole, a par 5. It was a bone dry and raised fairway, so he used discretion when driving across the farthest portions of the Bermuda-covered expanse. Observing Muunroe's dastardly deed, Stevie stopped his cart, stared intently, and screeched a reminder that it was indeed still "cart path only."

"Roger that, got it. Thanks for the memo."

Closer to the green, Muunroe again wandered onto the fairway, just far enough to violate the rule again. At this, our new-found buddy came over to innocent me and said, "Your buddy doesn't give a shit, does he? I'm finished."

"Huh, what? Finished from what?" I was clueless, thinking he had completed the hole before we had putted out.

After all, we were helping to speed up our play while doing no harm to the turf.

Nice guy Stevie suddenly transformed from Dr. Jekyll to Mr. Hyde as he drove away with a six-pack of our iced-down beverage. This could have been his plan all along—to steal our Bud Light at the first opportunity. Maybe he was in a hurry to finish the round. Maybe he had reached his maximum score for the day, much like an old-timer I knew, Robert Jenkins, who once said that he always shoots a score of 76. After watching Robert dissect his way to an eight on the first hole, followed by a seven, then another seven, I wondered how he could possibly be a near-scratch player. I received my answer when in the middle of the fairway on the twelfth hole; after having continued to play poorly, he picked up his ball and walked off the course.

"Boys," he announced, "I've reached my 76, and farther down the course than last week."

Stevie may have been influenced to hurry up by the golf course starter before the start of the round. Golf course managers all over the country try to get golfers to speed up play on the course, which is irritating and doesn't make sense to me. When the course conditions dictates that only the cart path be used, this contradicts the manager's wish that the golfers play quickly. Play can't move as fast when the golfers have to plod across the fairways to retrieve balls that were hit opposite the pathways. Under any condition, if a faster group is playing behind a slower group and is constantly kept waiting then etiquette and fair play says to let them through. Golf doesn't have a clocked time limit like football or soccer, nor should it.

It used to be that a group on a par-3 green would stop before putting and wave up the foursome behind to hit their shots. This seems like sound advice and gentlemanly conduct and should sustain the pace of play, but this courtesy has been discarded like yesterday's crumpled-up newspaper.

My old friend Robert Jenkins seems to have found the cure for slow play. It's simple, yet it's counter intuitive to the golfer's ego. Calmly pick up the ball when things get overwhelming, then move on. Your score might rise faster than an elevator in the Empire State Building, but you won't be guilty of slowing down play. Actually, anyone with an ego could benefit from this advice.

Only one caveat to this recommendation: Please don't drive off and leave with our cold beer.

CHAPTER 11

Oldham Daryl

DARYL LIVES A short distance, about a 9-iron shot for most of us, from the front porch of Mikey's house on the same street. Daryl is reminiscent of the TV character "Norm" from the Eighties show *Cheers*, the guy that everybody immediately likes, who has a permanent place on the corner stool at the bar. Whenever Mikey has friends over for drinks *après* golf in his front room, which doubles as a charming home bar and lounge, Daryl suddenly appears as though he had been listening from the outside of the house for just the right moment to enter, and take his rightful place on the corner stool of Mikey's bar and lounge.

Belinda, Mikey's delightful wife, dare I say a little nutty, too, for entertaining four, eventually five, with the entrance of Daryl, is always a gracious host to us tired, thirsty, and overwhelmingly hungry athletes. Scotty Dez refers to their place as his rest stop from the nearby interstate, a stop that is conveniently located halfway from Richmond to Virginia Beach where Scotty Dez and his wife travel to visit relatives on a fairly routine basis. But this is far better than your everyday

U.S. interstate rest area. Scotty Dez has spent the night as a houseguest and can attest to that.

The upscale house sits on the far end of a cul-de-sac in a quiet neighborhood, has a lengthy private driveway, and is entirely surrounded by woods. No lawn, only woods. If you happened to drive straight through the cul-de-sac down the driveway and veered off the paved road, you'd end up down a cliff in the woods, never to be seen or heard from again. The nearest neighbors, also in upscale houses, are far enough away that if you should want to murder someone and leave him or her in Mikey's forested backyard, no one would ever find the body. I'm not suggesting that anyone try that, but it occurred to me that it would be the ideal place to hide some-one. Or hide something, like a sack of money you "found" at the corner 7-Eleven.

Unlike an interstate stop, this rest stop is private and you have to know where it is. I doubt that even the other neigh-bors in the subdivision know the whereabouts of Mikey and Belinda's house. You could stop and ask the folks walking nearby for directions to Mikey and Belinda's house, but they would not be able to tell you. "I dunno, I know Mikey and Belinda well, they're likeable neighbors, but I'm not sure where their house is," the man walking his dog would inform you. "You could ask Daryl—he's the only person here who knows where their house is."

As you enter through the front porch with its pleasant swing-ing glider, a comfortable two-seater awaiting the weary travel-er, the bar is to the immediate right of the front door entrance. How convenient. Most homes in upscale communities have a small sitting room or library, perhaps a den to the right of the entryway, and I suppose this was the original purpose of the room. It is important and interesting to note here that there aren't any "downscale" houses or communities in America.

I'd categorize the merit of houses in this country in the following order: opulent, mansion-sized, upscale, middle class, poor, and poverty-stricken "hoods." Even those houses in the hoods have satellite TV with sixty-inch plasma or LCD screens, surround-sound, a stereo system with speakers containing woofers and tweeters, a PC with five trillion gigabytes of speed, and a new model SUV with twenty-inch rims and tires parked outside.

Mikey and Belinda's bar is a full service type of bar, with any kind of drink you could want. That is, when Mikey's serving. You can't just wander in there and order up a whiskey because, first of all, you have to know where the house is, and, secondly, Mikey might not be home. The room has an L-shaped wet bar with five stools, glasses hanging overhead on wooden racks with slats that allow for easy access to the glasses, a small refrigerator to store cold beverages, mostly bottled beer and a few cans of Pepsi; no Coke as his guests prefer Pepsi, and Mikey is always there for us—I mean, them, dimmed lighting for atmosphere, and a small TV up in one corner to watch the big game with friends. But rarely do guests watch anything, rockin' music fills the room instead. The unique sound system that Mikey installed himself lessens the allure of TV entertainment. With a click of the mouse, which is hooked up to the laptop, which is hooked into the stereo, which has small-yet-effective speakers hidden in each corner of the room, you can have "Satisfaction" by the Rolling Stones piped into the room. Or anything else you want, except Rap music.

Without warning or advance notice, his guests often break into song, ranging from "Yellow Submarine" to "Hotel California," or whatever they feel like singing that evening. It's not kara-oke, way too informal for that, although I must reveal that I once karaoked to "The Funky Cold Medina" at a bar far away from home where nobody knew me. There are more words to that song than I give credit to, and it was hard to keep up with the beat, if "You know wha' I'm sayin'." When singing that song, it comes down to style and attitude—if you cross your arms and bob your head with a slight tilt to the right, to the rhythm with the gansta lean, the inebriated audience will believe you got it right. "You know wha' I mean."

Near the floor of the bar itself, maybe six inches from the floor, there is a brass foot railing. The brass tubing was custom made and imported from Italy, we were told. Very nice touch, makes the seating more comfortable when your feet aren't dangling from the front of the stool. Mikey requires a cover charge from Daryl to enter the bar, which equates to a single activity—polishing the brass with Brasso liquid once a month. At least he doesn't have to sweep and mop the floors too.

Daryl, in his late forties is a non-golfer, mainly because he spends a great amount of time at his dream job (heck, every-one's dream job) as Quality Control Specialist and supervisor at one of the largest beer breweries in America. Maybe it is *the* largest brewery, I'll have to look it up to be sure. Oh, what the hell, just call it the largest brewery in America and prob-ably the entire universe. As with most hardworking folks, he didn't start out as a supervisor, he began as a dedicated em-ployee in the role of deliveryman. You've seen these drivers with their huge 18 wheelers—semi-tractors and trailers taking up two thirds of the parking lot at 7-Eleven or parked stationary in front of a store like Wal-Mart, blocking the entrance and exit doors for hours. Daryl started out as one of those delivery guys.

Now that Daryl has progressed to a more important position, I'm not saying that delivery drivers aren't important, I'm just saying he was promoted to supervisor, hence he's not satisfied with just being "Daryl." Daryl is a nice name as names go, but let's be direct here, it is kind of bland, and even he admits this. It's a lot like having a hot fudge sundae with vanilla ice cream in a cup, but without the hot fudge and whipped cream over it. The ice cream is good, but where is the pizzazz? The name Daryl is good, but not memorable, like the sundae without the hot fudge and whipped cream.

(Suddenly, I'm hungry—I feel like a quick trip to Dairy Queen.)

So, Daryl was bored with his name and was concerned about the blandness it evoked. One evening sitting at Mikey's place, we tried to help him out, coming up with alternatives to his given name: Dumbass, Sonofabitch, Stupid Shit—but, to our surprise, he didn't care for those. "How about 'Non-Golfing Neighbor from Oldham Street'" was Belinda's input. Very sweet, Belinda, but a little too long. Some of it resonated though, and Daryl thought it clever, so it was shortened to "Oldham Street Daryl," and later just to "Oldham Daryl." Oldham Daryl with his updated name has become "the most interesting man in the world." Perhaps not the most interesting, but certainly the most welcome after he stocks Mikey's bar with complimentary cases of cold beer provided by the biggest brewery in America. It is often said, and worth repeating here, "You can take the man from delivery, but you can't take the delivery from the man."

Oldham Daryl worked his way up from deliveryman and truck driver to head honcho inside the brewery. He progressed to Ingredient Specialist, the person with the important job of adding the exact amount of hops, barley, wheat, and whatever else goes into beer making. This is all dumped into an enormous vat of heated water, which is then stirred by the Mixer Specialist. The Mixer Specialist is one step higher than the Ingredient Specialist, since the water and added ingredients have to blend just right for the right amount of time, or else you end up with a batch of beer soup with the consistency of watered-down mashed potatoes. Nobody in America, especially any Southern Country Gentleman or Redneck, would stand for that.

Watching the Mixer Specialist is the Timer Specialist, whose job it is to walk up and down the beer corridors with stopwatch and calendar in hand to log the times required for each vat to turn and mix everything. Undercooked beer, according to the Timer Specialist, gets labeled as "Light Beer" and is sent off in one direction to be inspected and tasted. Overcooked beer becomes "Dark Beer" after it turns a distinctive dark brownish color if the heat is too high or it is cooked too long. It too is sent off in another direction and is inspected and sampled before being labeled and placed in brown bottles. The majority of the beer that's completed in the perfect amount of time is the main product for the brewery and given the brewery's "golden label," thought to suit nearly everyone's taste.

I learned this firsthand from Oldham Daryl, who has worked at the brewery since he was fifteen.

The brewery has created many jobs in America and has helped the unemployment rate to remain fairly low, relatively speaking. Relative to countries without any kind of significant beer breweries, that is. We can't compete with Germany in this regard, as they have breweries on nearly every street corner over there, much like we have 7-Elevens or gas station convenience stores over here. Unlike in the United States, though, their operators aren't named Patel or Abdulla.

You can imagine that there are many jobs in a brewery, and while I can't name them all here, I know there is a Light Beer Specialist, a Dark Beer Specialist, a Regular Beer Specialist, and at least one Brew Master overseeing those specialists. There is also a Quality Control Specialist for each type and brand of beer made by that individual brewery. Don't forget the Label Maker for each beer, who applies the label on the correct side of the bottle and at the correct angle, the Bottling Expert who has to know the correct bottle for each type of beer, the Can Expert for the same reason, the Quart Size Bottling Expert, the Keg Expert, and the Taste Test Expert. Oldham Daryl is the Quality Control Supervisor and monitor of all the beer types at the brewery, and the one person you can thank or cuss about depending on the flavor of your beverage. In Middle America, he has more influence and holds a more important position than any of our elected political figures.

Although Mikey doesn't work in the beer-making industry, he knows nearly as much as Oldham Daryl about mixing and drinking cocktails. For Mikey, the mixologist, every alcoholic beverage is a cocktail to him. On most nights at Mikey's, after several cocktails, the conversation turns to politics and political correctness in our country. Not a politician, he nevertheless has strong and resolute feelings about politics. This is evidenced by Belinda's one-eyed cat he named Reagan.

Reagan, a three-year-old Persian was blind in his left eye since birth. Laying at your feet near the bar stool, he appears docile and normal. He doesn't move much except to retrieve pretzel crumbs dropped from above his hunkered down space. When he does wander away, he tends to bump into objects on his left side. He nudges the leg of the table and inadvertently stumbles as he rounds the room's corner heading to the kitchen. His body leans to the right favoring the side where his sight is clearer. Reagan doesn't complain with harsh screeches or mild meows if he crashes into an unanticipated piece of furniture. He has never uttered a sound in his young life, his vocal cords unable to produce a whisper. His mouth protrudes with an oversize bulging top lip, which makes him look like he is constantly pouting. It looks a bit like former heavyweight boxer Joe Frazier after he was repeatedly popped in the mouth by Mohamed Ali.

Some guys' golf games are meant to go haywire when influenced by outside forces. Thus is the case with Mikey, I realized one afternoon. If you want to screw up his "round of the century," then mention politics and how the current officials have messed up locally and nationally. Without naming any politician in particular, Mikey's temper flares as he begins to flail his arms at the slightest hint of political discussion.

"What do you think of our Congressman?" His face turns grim as he smacks his driver against the ground.

"What is your solution to the high federal taxes?" He slams his club into his bag with a loud "Grrrrr" heard around the course.

"Which of the Democrats do you favor for our next President? Which Republican do you like?" He stalks around looking for his ball stroked into the weeds no more than one hundred forty yards away. If the ball travels left, he blames the Democrats. If the ball goes right, he blames the Republicans. If the ball is hit down the middle, he says it is the will of the Independents.

Mikey always needs help in locating his ball, regardless of how far it went. On more than one occasion he has blamed his companions for not watching his ball—a breach of etiquette, he claims. My favorite reaction from Scotty Dez—"We are all Libertarians, so we don't care about the whereabouts of your ball, just as long as you don't regulate it."

If you're ever in the neighborhood, Mikey and Belinda's house is worth the stop for some fine cocktails, good humor, friendly conversation, eclectic music (excluding Rap), golf highlights, and beer-making details. And you will get to meet Oldham Daryl; that is, if you can find your way to the house hidden in the woods.

CHAPTER **12**

The Hurricanes

THE HURRICANES HIGH school team was into the second hour of their first practice of the summer golfing season when a young teenage black girl asked the question, "Coach, which side of the club head do I hit the ball with?" To her this was a serious question, and I answered it with thoughtful consideration. None of the other twelve students joked or laughed about it. Remarkably, a few of the others may have had the same question in their minds.

She was gripping the club as I had instructed and was swinging the 7-iron like a pendulum in front of her in order to get the feel of the club. After my basic introductory lesson consisting of proper grip, grip pressure, stance, posture, alignment, and swing takeaway, the question arose. This was my second season as volunteer golf coach at this predominantly minority-centered high school. During the previous year, the team was a startup of seven young students, all extreme beginners. Only four students made it through the three-month long summer session that kicked off in July. The game was too demanding, they had decided.

The school, a modern facility with a full complement of teachers, faculty, and administrators, also had a complete athletic program. Teams were successful on the football gridiron and on the basketball courts. They also dominated the ten-school league in tennis. Golf was in a shambles, however, having never finished a season out of the basement in league standings. For at least half of the previous eight seasons, they hadn't fielded a team at all.

The golf "program," if you will, had one and a half sets of clubs and two useable golf bags. The clubs were old, many bent at the shafts, with grips that would tear the skin off your hands. The putters were cast-offs from a local putt-putt miniature course, mainly short and crooked with flat heads of different colors. Of the two golf bags, just three pocket zippers were zipper-able. After contacting a few golfing friends over e-mail and phone, I was able to make upgrades and significant improvements to the equipment.

With their like-new donated clubs, bags, and balls, the team was now ready to take on the competition. Huddling the team together prior to their first-ever tournament match against the nine other high schools in the area, we went over last-minute preparations. "Make sure you know what brand of ball you're playing, and make your identifying marks on each of them now," I insisted.

"I marked mine last night at home, so I'd be ready for today," exclaimed Rasheed with wide gaping smile.

"Very good, let me see your marks," I answered.

During one of our practices I explained that since golf balls look similar when seen from a distance, it is important to place individual marks on the ball with a sharpie pen having permanent indelible ink. The marks could consist of small dots or the golfer's initials as well as other unobtrusive renderings. To demonstrate, I showed the team my golf ball marked with a single green dot under the ball name and its imprinted number.

Rasheed carefully opened his sleeve of three golf balls. As delightful as a child opening wrapped Christmas gifts on Christmas morning, he displayed his colorful handiwork. They were all completely covered in a deep purple as though someone had dipped them in a can of Sherwin-Williams semi-gloss house paint.

"Wow, you kinda went overboard on these," I gasped, holding the enlarged Concord grape looking objects.

"But this third one isn't completely covered, you got about seventy-five percent of it."

"Yeah, sorry coach, I hope that one is useable, I ran out of ink before I could finish it." Rasheed grinned proudly.

"I am sure these balls conform to the many rules of golf for tournament play," I assured him, even though I wasn't completely convinced.

"It doesn't appear you have altered the natural components of the ball, it is still round, a suitable tournament brand, and you haven't enhanced its' capability. It certainly cannot be considered a training aid when used for play. You will be the only player with purple balls today," as I shook my head, looked skyward and silently mouthed the words, 'why me, Lord?'

Each player was given a sleeve of school-issued "Top Flites." During earlier practice rounds they had used a mix of other brands, too. Each teenager was asked to name the type of ball they planned to use.

"Coach, I have Top Flite number 4," responded Ja'Quan.

"Coach, I think mine is Top Flite number 2, I colored over the number with my ink," Rasheed said.

"I have _Fitlist_ number 2," offered Naje.

"Hmmm, that one is unusual; don't think I've ever seen that brand before, Naje," I commented. Looking at the Titleist ball, I realized he had interpreted the "T" in the cursive font as an Old English "F." Hence, "Fitlist." Not to worry   that one was lost promptly on the second hole in the high weeds way off the fairway. Now someone else is probably toting around his "Fitlist" ball.

The damages after just one round of tournament golf were extraordinary. Two broken drivers, one headless 3-wood, one bent 5-iron shaft, 30 lost golf balls. The 3-wood had been destroyed on the driving range before play even began.

"Coach, that was my favorite club," Jamel moaned, as the head flew further than the ball off the driving range mat. Others watched in amazement, noticing that the trajectory of his shot was the straightest it had been all day.

"Sorry, Tiger, I guess I should have mentioned for the tenth time not to hit the ground first before making contact with the ball," I half-jokingly answered. "Besides, how could that be your favorite club when you just picked it up for the first time three days ago?"

Only six golfers are needed to make a team to play in a high school match. With ten tournament matches on the schedule, I predicted that the team would certainly run out of balls and most of the clubs too. It was a good thing these youngsters were not equipment testers for the major manufacturers of new clubs and balls.

"Ah, this new Nike is no good—the driver head snaps off too easy when I smash it into the turf," one such student tester might report.

"These forty-eight dollar-per-dozen Bridgestones are lost too frequently," another tester would remark. "Not recommended."

To round out the testing feedback, Naje' would offer, "Do not play Titleist—the scripted label is too hard to read."

At the high school tournaments, adults volunteer to assist the coaches during the course of play. At one tournament at the prestigious Kiskiack Golf Club in Williamsburg, Virginia, Ken Olsen, an older gentleman, offered his time as a volunteer. He was cardboard thin with crinkled eyes and spiky whitish hair protruding from under his wide brim farmers' woven straw sweat-stained hat that was haphazardly cocked to one side of his head. His drab clothes were so crumpled it looked like they were shot from a wrinkle gun. He had the wild-eyed look of Albert Einstein and with a PhD in aerodynamics; Ken Olsen was a retired space engineer. A career Rocket Scientist from NASA with forty years of experience, he was the lead scientist for the propulsion of the lunar module landing craft and also aided in the development of the highly successful space shuttle. He received Presidential accolades thru the years for his achievements in space exploration research. Grounded on planet Earth, on the other hand, he was lost.

Ken arrived with a half dozen walkie-talkies for the coaches to use to communicate the players' scores and the progression of play. These would've been a valuable tool for the coaches to monitor each foursome of the tournament. However, the devices' batteries were dead and they were therefore unusable. Ken was somehow unaware that batteries not used in spaceships have to be recharged and tested before their use.

As the tournament progressed, Ken was asked to drive his cart to Hole #5 where the path intersects with Hole #15, considered an ideal location to observe the players. Here he could watch the pace of play on both the front nine and back nine of the course. At this vantage point he could assist any golfers in need and offer advice on the golf rules. But Ken, our PhD friend, never arrived at his designated location. Throughout the afternoon he was seen riding back and forth, primarily in front of the clubhouse and between Holes #1 and #10 where both teeing grounds begin play on the front and back nines.

"What happened?" a team coach asked.

"I lost my vector," was Ken's reply. "It seems my navigational tracking system was disrupted."

"Oh, can't let that happen. Just follow this paved path and you should make it."

"I did find two odd colored golf balls way off in the woods on the third hole," Ken remarked. "At first I thought they were purple wild berries, so I picked them up and discovered they are golf balls."

An hour after play had ended for the day, Ken was unaccounted for. He was last seen roaming the pathways surrounding fairways 12 and 13.

The practices continued throughout the season and the beginners progressed. At one point Rasheed asked, "Coach, what is it called when the ball rolls into the cup? Is it a homerun?"

"No, Rasheed, believe it or not, it is stated as being 'in the cup' and is given a number, as in how many strokes it took to get there. If it is a hole-in-one on a par 3 hole, it is referred to as an ace. If it is two less than par, it is an eagle. If it is one under par, it is a birdie. If it is one over par, it is a bogey. And if it is two over par, it is a double bogey."

"Thanks, Coach. Then I wonder what my score of nine would be called?"

"It would be called a lousy score," I said, reassuring him with a quick smile.

During a practice round, Ja'Quan was on the first tee holding his driver up perpendicularly between his right index finger and thumb while squinting at the fairway ahead. With quizzical intrigue, another player asked, "What are you doing, Ja'Quan?"

"I'm sizing up the location of my drive. I saw one of the pros at a tournament on TV do this, so I thought I'd try."

"Save it for the green with putter in hand," I explained, "We don't need to plumb-bob with a driver. Find a target in the distance and aim for it." I've never witnessed anyone plumb-bobbing on the tee, except for that day.

The teenagers tried to learn the game and seemed to enjoy their time on the course. Mostly they enjoyed the snacks, sandwiches, fruit, and Gatorade offered to them after the practices and matches. To their credit, they eagerly accepted the many challenges posed by the sport. Oftentimes parents and friends of the players were unable to drive the distance to the practices or tournaments due to their summer work schedules. But two of the kids traveled twenty miles on city buses to find their way to the practice course. With bags of clubs slung over their shoulders, they boarded the bus on the east end of the city at 8 a.m., changed buses two times, and walked the final two miles to the clubhouse that was set back in the city of Newport News in the parks area. They were never late for our 11 a.m. start of practice. On one such journey, the Park Ranger interrupted their progress as they were heading off in the wrong direction through the park. She delivered them to the course, even though taxi service is not a Ranger duty. After practice, I dropped them off at the nearest bus stop for the return. The two youngsters made the trip a complete day. They appreciated a sport filled with nature, comradery, and leisure.

In our second season of tournament play, the Hurricanes moved up the leaderboard into ninth place. No trophies were handed out, but the satisfaction of learning the basics and the fun of competing seemed good enough for them. These youngsters learned a great amount of golf techniques and skills required for play. They also learned about sportsmanship, friendship, and generosity. They learned that hard work and effort does have rewards in the end. They are a dedicated bunch of kids who vowed to return next season and ready to improve.

Despite Ken Olsen's ineffectiveness, he nevertheless volunteered his time and interest in helping young people. Volunteers are needed in every aspect of society, so it was comforting to have Ken on location, orbiting the clubhouse.

And I let him keep his two wildly-colored purple souvenirs.

CHAPTER 13

The Sounds of Freedom

IN MY LIFETIME I have played golf on many military bases across the United States and overseas. The military has taken me from New York to Hawaii and to states in between, and at each location, golf was an important part of social and recreational life. I learned to play on the course right in the middle of Schofield Barracks, Hawaii, which is right in the middle of the island of Oahu. Membership dues in the 1970s were a whopping eight dollars per month for my pay grade, and for that we played on two eighteen-hole courses and one nine-hole course. Walking was free and riding in a cart cost five dollars for the round. Walking was the better option since it was good physical exercise, despite what the critics claim. Those who walk four to five miles during a round of golf inevitably win out over those who sit on the couch and criticize the game.

The course at Schofield was flat and circumvented obstacles in the form of warehouse buildings, barracks, and office buildings. On that course, I usually played to 3-over; that is, one over the warehouse, one over the road, and one over the fence. Hole #5 was a prime example of the complexity and narrowness of the course layout. Hole #5, a straightaway par 4 was lined on its left by a straight main road leading up and over Kole Kole Pass. Kole Kole is the saddle in the abbreviated mountain range where the Japanese flew their bombers at low altitude to be undetected by radar to start American involvement in World War II in the Pacific. They didn't bother to drop bombs on the golfers on that Sunday morning; instead they headed toward Wheeler Airfield nearby and on to Pearl Harbor. Relatively speaking, that's a good thing too—a golfer who misses a shot due to a sudden loud noise can become instantly annoyed and wildly upset. I once watched legendary pro golfer Raymond Floyd stare down a spectator who was about to take his picture while he was putting at a tournament in Myrtle Beach, South Carolina. Raymond, hearing the camera's shutter click from roughly fifty yards away, pointed with his wavering putter and growled directly at the offending guy. All else was silent around the green, but the nanosecond click of the camera lens sent the golfer into a frenzy. Even today when playing with friends, I'm startled by the whirring sound of a gas engine leaf blower that is one thousand yards away on a street several blocks from the fairway. Noises like those always manage to distract us amateurs, and we can't do much to stop the madness like pros can. There are many annoying sounds, but the belching roar of engines and the sight of three hundred Japanese Zeros overhead must have ruined many swings at Schofield Barracks that day.

That same road, Kole Kole Highway, is one where infantry soldiers make their way around the compound during road march training. A severe hook driven to the left of the fairway and rough would place the marchers with their forty-pound rucksacks, helmets, and rifles at the ready position in the line of golf ball fire. Fortunately, I never hit one of the soldiers during their training, mainly because my slice carried the ball in the opposite direction, over Hawaiian pine trees, and over the chain link fence protecting the fairway's right side where the pineapple fields awaited. The eight-foot high chain link fence with barbed wire strung across the top in three layers skirted the right side of hole #5. The managers of the Dole Pineapple Company realized this and turned a profit on harvesting and canning their product from that field, and by re-selling hundreds of misdirected golf balls discovered by their field workers.

That wasn't the only obstacle found on the course. At a different hole, another par 4 with a 90-degree dogleg that angled down the right of a generous-enough fairway, many golfers attempted to cut distance by hitting over the corner. A metal one-story warehouse stood in the way, positioned exactly at the edge of the dogleg. A carry of 230 yards would clear the roof but many shots did not. The metal siding and rusted metal sloping roof had been pelted with so many dents and rounded-out scrapes that NASA considered practicing their moon landings with lunar modules on the warehouse craters. The shot heard 'round the course was a distinctive hollow boom as though a bass drum had been smacked with a hammer each time a golf ball echoed off Building 415.

Large military trucks roamed across the center of the course, creating an unmistakable grumbling diesel engine roar that was made worse by the exhaust smoke and dust kicked up by the oversized tactical tires. Farther up the road, the artillery teams practiced their live fire into the mountain range during their training days, which were often. The 105mm cannons shot projectiles far enough away from the main part of the base, but it was still loud enough to disrupt the whispering sounds of the ever-present trade winds sweeping across the island, entering the eardrums of soldiers and golfers alike. Training continued on Saturdays and Sunday afternoons, prime time for golf, and prime training time for the Reserve Army Units stationed in Hawaii. The unrelenting crack of the cannons and their impacts seemed to be timed to the exact moment the golfer started his backswing. The sounds were distinctive and loud, heard across the area for miles. As one senior enlisted NCO, with flattop military style crewcut, older-than-dirt Army Command Sergeant Major explained to me and my partners, "You are listening to the Sounds of Freedom."

There was a different sound on the other military course I played on, as part of my membership trio. On the Kalakaua Championship course, muffled noises could be heard in the distance since it was a few miles from the one at Schofield Barracks. Kalakaua, set in and surrounded by the serenity of the rolling pineapple fields, created a calm feeling of relaxation. No trucks, no troops passing by with their chants of cadence, no artillery to jitter the nerves. An occasional "pop-pop-pop" of rifle fire from a distant field-training site used by the infantry and supporting cast was preferable to the banging of artillery and mortars flying over your position on the fairway. Kalakaua was a tough championship course, explaining why amateur tournaments were routinely scheduled there. During one such tournament of individual play, my companion and I were playing terribly by any standards and way above our handicaps as we shuffled along in the unusually humid conditions. On the final hole, I allowed my partner a "gimme" of three feet, thinking that since we were both so far down the leaderboard, one less stroke wouldn't matter to either of our scores. The scoundrel beat me out for third place in our flight by one stroke and won a nice prize, while I won a lesson for a lifetime of golfing.

The third course rounding out the membership was a nifty 9-hole layout on Ft. Shafter. This was a walker's course, no riding carts permitted on the premises. Each hole was uphill making the course tougher than it showed on the scorecard. It was situated on the lava-based edge of the Diamond Head volcanic crater that had formed the island thousands of years ago. There were two sets of tees, so a different one was played for the "back 9." Not much in the way of outside disturbances there because Ft. Shafter was the home of the Army's Personnel Center in the Pacific Command. If you listened rather intently, you could hear the "click, click, click" sound of rapid-fire typewriters from the open office building windows. In the distance and over some hills was Tripler Army Hospital, set up even higher on the side of the volcano overlooking the ocean below. MEDEVAC, UH1H "Huey" helicopters would circle the emergency room helipad before their touchdown, and the distinctive "whop, whop, whop" of their rotor blades made for an eerie, distant echo. The Ft. Shafter course was a short distance from downtown Honolulu and a comfortable getaway for quick rounds of golf before hitting the nightclub scene of Waikiki.

On the northern outskirts of Honolulu is a little-known course at Barber's Point Naval Air Station. From the first tee, golfers hear the engine bellows as pilots crank up the F4 Phantom all-purpose jets on the runway nearby. The F4s were the workhorse aircraft flown during the Vietnam era, and pilots continue to practice their skills in these iconic planes. The Barber's Point course is situated on a forgotten, ancient runway, once an extension of the commercial airport. The ground is hard, made of compacted soil and feels like concrete under your golf spikes. And, of course, it is concrete or tarmac that remained in place as the course was developed for the Navy Aviators. They needed a place to play, and once the Honolulu International Airport grew in popularity as a destination, it expanded to the edges of the Naval Air Station with a newer, improved runway utilized by the larger jets offering classier service to the islands. The former runway was allotted to the Barber's Point neighbor.

On the fairway off hole #9, commercial 747 jumbo jets have their very own extended taxiway with an overpass leading to the main runway. I have never been that close to the underbelly of an enormous jet in motion. I waved to, and saluted, the pilots in the cockpit as they gave the "thumbs up" sign while passing overhead. The jet was close enough that the wingspan created a shadow over the golfers standing below. Waving to the passengers observing me from their window seats, I could see the frowns on their faces as they probably wished they were standing where we were on the fairway instead of leaving that tropical paradise.

Being assigned to Hawaii's Hickam Air Force Base has to be every Airman's and Air Force pilot's dream come true. Hickam, a chip shot from Honolulu, serves as the military cargo hub for the west. From the windswept golf course, where palm trees bend like frozen question marks in the prevailing westerly winds, gigantic Air Force C-141s, C-5s and larger cargo carriers fly overhead, resembling pterodactyls of the dinosaur age. These flying predators make loud, yet hushed, sounds as they maneuver through the soft breezes. Hickam, a tough course, plays mostly into the wind and becomes even tougher if your ball skirts onto the runway and is sucked up by the engine of a giant jet, then spit out like the pea soup rejected by an infant. Not only is your shanked shot enormously out of bounds and irretrievable, but one step toward the edge will have the SPs (Security Police) jumping on your cart bag with their bayonets extended. You'll hear the sirens and see their blue lights from as far away as neighboring Maui as you are escorted off the air base. Your new destination will be to a desolate island without sunshine.

One of the most scenic views of any military course has to be from the Navy-Marine Course overlooking Pearl Harbor. By overlooking, I mean directly on the hillside up from the green-blue waters of the horseshoe-shaped Pearl Harbor inlet. The view from many of the tee boxes includes the outline of the battleship Arizona and its Memorial. Maybe it was intended to be that way, as a gloomy reminder of the sacrifices made by the sailors of an earlier time. The course itself is considered the "grand-daddy" of military courses on the island. Lush, always green fairways, ocean breezes, swaying palms, and tropical-smelling flowers make up the essence of the place. It caters to all ranks of the military, but caters more so to the higher ranks, I found out. The higher the rank, the better the tee time, especially on weekends when the brass have most of their free time. The management would've never agreed to that, nor would it be publicized as the policy, but I often tested it out. In the Army, a Captain is an important rank at company grade level, but a Captain in the Navy is a much higher grade, equivalent to an Army Colonel, a senior grade level. A Colonel is one step below a General, as is a Navy Captain one step below an Admiral. Calling the pro shop to schedule for my foursome never resulted in an ideal starting time. To get a decent tee time, I asked my Army Captain friend to schedule for me, giving his true name and rank, Captain Newman. "No problem, sir, you got it," said the pro shop employee. We had broken the unwritten code. However, after showing our ID cards once inside the pro shop, our secret was revealed as the manager sneered, stared at, and inspected our youthful appearances. He was a retired Navy Captain and we had outmaneuvered him. Or as former President George W. Bush once said, we had used "strategery."

In the middle of the United States is an Army training center stuck out in the Missouri countryside, Fort Leonard Wood. Because of its remote location soldiers assigned there have affectionately nicknamed it *Fort Lost-In-the-Woods*. This base is an enormous Army Engineer training site, where hundreds of soldiers are trained each year on the heavy construction equipment used by Combat Engineers. You can hear the rumble of D-5 bulldozers, road scrapers, backhoes, front-end bucket loaders and oversize dump trucks miles away in the countrified air. Soldiers practice moving dirt piles around in the "million dollar hole" training area, named for the amount and cost of equipment located within the pit. Hearing these distant sounds it feels as if you are standing next to a diesel truck continually idling throughout your four-and-one-half hour golf outing. The golf course is adjacent to the Big Piney River down in a hollow where sounds are absorbed. The Big Piney, isn't big at all in this location, but the swooshing waters of the low class one rapids when you get near helps to offset the diesel truck sounds.

On the east coast, in New York State, there is a delightful eighteen-hole course at the United States Military Academy at West Point. There are plenty of hills and tree-lined fairways, as well as a few rock outcroppings to avoid, as the course is located near Bear Mountain State Park and the mighty Catskills. One of the par-5 holes climbs up from the tee and drops practically straight down in the opposing direction, a drop of over one hundred feet in elevation, which levels off to the green some six hundred yards from the start. The hole becomes part of the "bunny slope" for skiing novices in the snowy months. But it is hole #8 where the action takes place. Aligning the fairway beyond a row of maples, oaks, and hemlocks to the right is a rough country back road that leads to a training camp in the hills. Soldiers and Cadets, soon to be Lieutenants, march this road frequently. Summer months are the primary training months for the Cadets, soon to be Lieutenants. You can hear their cadence and "Jody Songs" through the echoing canyon of leafy branches as they serenade the bystanders on the fairway.

"Jody, Jody don't be blue, the Army's here and we're comin' through. Jody, Jody were you been? Over to the Point and back again. Sound off, one, two, hit it again, three, four, bring it on home, one, two, three, four; three, four."

"Jody" has been around for fifty years or more and sung by every soldier, officer, and Cadet, soon to be Lieutenant over the years. I doubt that Jody was ever in the Army or any other military branches because platoons don't sing about people they know.

They'd often sing about Army stuff, too.

"They say that in the Army, the food is mighty fine, a biscuit rolled off the table and killed a friend of mine."

"They say that in the Army the coffee is mighty fine, it looks like dirty oil and tastes like turpentine."

A severe banana-shaped slice will carry the golf ball from hole #8 through and over the trees and into that song-filled road where the Cadets, soon to be Lieutenants, are headed toward you. I know this from personal experience. One such orbit of my partner's traveled that way, only to be hurled back quickly and precisely. Muffled laughter ensued from the platoon comprised of forty men and women, and my theory is that one of those Cadets, soon to be Lieutenant, will make a fine Infantry Officer based on the accuracy of the ball's trajectory, which was much like a mortar round or far-flung hand grenade. My partner had the last laugh; he saved a stroke plus distance based on USGA rule number one, "a ball is played where it lies," and rule number 924b(a4), "a ball thrown back into the fairway by an unknown source, or known source such as a Cadet, soon to be Lieutenant, is meant to be played where it lies."

Salutes were exchanged between the Platoon Leader and us four guys. The Platoon got an unexpected humorous break in their monotonous task of chanting while marching, and we all had Army tunes humming in our heads throughout the rest of the day. *"Jody, Jody, don't be blue…"*

Farther south down the east coast are two "sister courses" at the Ft. Eustis Army and Langley Air Force Bases in Virginia. They are joined by the title: Joint Base Langley, Eustis, or JBLE.

The Pines at Eustis is a twenty-seven-hole layout bordered by the Warwick River, which offers interesting waterfront and marsh views along several holes. Across from the entrance to the course is Felker Army Airfield, an active place for Army Aviation. Very active, with the continual "thwhop, thwhop, thwhop" sound of the CH1D models of the Chinook twin-engine cargo helicopters hovering directly overhead. With their two engines that emit an excruciating whine and larger rotor blades in the front and back, their "thwopping" noise is louder than the distinctive "whopping" from the Huey. The aviators bank and turn directly over the course, practicing their pilot skills. They are so loud and so low, you'd expect a squad of Airborne Rangers to rappel out and onto the eighteenth green and to take up a surrounding defensive posture, weapons drawn.

Dissecting the center of the Pines course is the Army's railway which surrounds the lower half of Fort Eustis. The main track intersects with the golf cart path in two locations, and runs parallel to holes two, three, sixteen and seventeen. The train runs frequently with its five thousand ton diesel-electric bright red locomotive with ten boxcars and caboose coupled behind. This mainline is used for practice and trial runs by train engineers for their operator's certification. As the train rumbles through the swampy and forested remote locations of the base, it can be heard in the distance for a mile or more. You can feel the ground shake under your spikes as the heavy metal cylindrical wheels squeal and pound over the rusted six foot gauge track as the train approaches. The *clickety-clack, clickety clack* entices all who hear it to stop and take in the wonderment. The engineer yanks defiantly on the cord that projects the locomotive's harsh warning whistle. First one short blast, followed by two more prior to crossing an intersection. The third, a long blast as the train is upon the cart path, each warning a required part of train operations. At the intersections, there aren't automatic gates that clunk down to stop pedestrian traffic, although the path has warning lights and the *ding, ding, ding* reminders to halt. It is understandable that three-putt bogeys are commonplace on the adjoining holes.

The Langley Air Force Base Eaglewood Club is equally as frightening or even more so, fittingly given the menacing name of Raptor Course. Located twenty minutes from its "sister," the Raptor is surrounded by the real Raptors, F-22 all weather, all purpose, all everything Mach 5 rapid response jetfighters. The runway is adjacent to the clubhouse entrance. Every day the jets scramble for immediate action in the skies above. This is not practice. I'm not giving away any military secrets when I tell you that they screech down the nearby runway in pairs, creating jet noise in Dolby surround-sound stereo in hundreds of decibels. The Raptors sound like Godzilla versus Rodan when they fought over Tokyo. The ultimate, undisputable, untamed "champion dragon" is on the far side of the course at the NASA complex where they test rockets for space missions. NASA shares a back entrance gate with the Air Force Base. Throughout the day a large air pressure chamber that looks like one giant funnel connected to another lying on its side expels horrendous air-belching screams alien to the human race. The locals have nicknamed it "the Dragon," from which the interval of sounds cannot be timed. The indiscriminate decibels emanating from this monster shake the ground, make the whole body quiver, and disrupt a backswing without warning.

Once the Raptors and the Dragon have passed and your pulse rate has returned to normal, you'll soon hear the Air Combat Command Base Headquarters broadcast the Air Force song over their loudspeakers, which happens at noon each day. Unless you're associated with the Air Force, you probably know the catchy tune but not the words.

"Doot-de-do, do,do,do,do,do, do-de-doot, do, do de-do, da, da, da, de-do." And you can hum along with the rhythmic musical while strolling down the ninth fairway.

Another feature is the sound of the five o'clock "Retreat" blasted all over the base at the end of the day. The two JBLE bases are known for this daily tribute, which signifies the end of daily activities. It is customary to halt and render the proper acknowledgements toward the American flag as it is lowered at Base headquarters. You'll be unable to see the flag, but you'll hear the music carrying through the air. It is a humbling reminder to stop, stand at attention, and remove your golf cap with hand over heart. The SPs or MPs (Military Police) will not be observing you from beyond the cluster of bushes up ahead, ready to haul you off if you violate these military customs and courtesies. But if there is a Senior NCO in sight, he will holler from across two fairways and race over to drag you to the ground, screaming while you knock out twenty pushups for ignoring this basic Code of Military Courtesy.

Just east of these monsters, no more than a forty-mile jaunt, is Battlefield Golf Course in Virginia Beach, Virginia. Not technically a military course located on a military compound, it is close enough. Named "Battlefield" due to the Civil War battles claimed to have been once fought there, the course features miniature Civil War replica cannons marking each tee location. It should have replicas of five hundred pound bombs instead. The ominous factor is that this course lies directly in the path of the Naval Aviation Fentress Field, a practice facility for touch 'n go fighter aircraft. The sound is so ear-splitting that I'm surprised the starter doesn't hand out earmuffs to all unsuspecting newcomers. The F-18 Hornet pilots practice landing on and taking off from naval vessels, although there are no aircraft carriers on dry land. Thank goodness they are only practicing as they fly their jets at tree-top level, buzzing close to the ant-like figures below, who scramble to get out of harm's way. Luckily, the only actual harm is to your ears, as the deafening sound is worse than standing beside the tallest speakers in the front row of a Metallica concert. As the thunder- jet fighters come unrelenting in waves, they turn on their laser lights and lock in on targets below. Golfers and their carts are the intended targets. Looking up, you can see the bomb pods and fuselage underneath the wings, which makes even the most hardened military Vet squat down, jump into the nearest ravine and take cover. In a discussion I had with two of these Top Gun jet jockeys, they admitted to placing their bomb-sights and lasers on the folks below, because after all, "We are only practicing for the real missions."

This course is number one in the order of merit for the noisiest, loudest, unforgiving, and most unpleasant location in the U.S.

This cacophony of sounds, from the "thwop, thwop, thwop" of choppers, to the roar of the Raptors, Dragons, and jet engines, to bulldozers and engineer road machines, to the cadence of Army chants and songs, to the booming sounds of artillery and mortars and diesel trucks passing by, and the thundering of oversized locomotives with railcars attached, it is still reassuring to realize that what you are essentially hearing are this nation's "Sounds of Freedom."

CHAPTER **14**

Mulligans

A YOUNG AMERICAN golfer was playing for the first time at the home of golf, the Old Course in St. Andrews, Scotland. From the first tee, nervous with knees and legs shaking like chilled Jell-O that had not quite solidified, he dubbed his drive which landed no more than sixty-five yards from the teeing ground into the right rough. He re-teed, then took his allocated Mulligan and was quite satisfied with the second shot that resulted in far better distance and location on the fairway. Smiling and turning to his Scottish playing partners, locals to the area, gentlemen and scholars of the game, he remarked, "In America, a second shot from the first tee is called a Mulligan. What do you call it over here?"

Without hesitation, foregoing wit or charm they chided, "Here we call it 'lying three,' young laddie."

Every reasonable amateur knows what it means to be able to take a "Mulligan." The Mulligan is supposed to correct the first errant tee shot on the very first hole of the day. This usually happens because you rushed to the first tee and did not warm up beforehand on the driving range or putting green. It can also be agreed upon by the members of your four-some to take the Mulligan at some other needed or precisely-timed shot during the round. Amateurs aren't perfect; they can sometimes use an extra crutch to get them through their round. Let's be honest, amateurs abhor the thought of practicing and warming up on the range before moving to the first tee. "Gotta save those good shots for the course, not waste them on the practice range," they say.

It is in this vein of thought that I present to you some figurative Mulligans, tangential thoughts shanked away from the previous chapters.

Golf publications are an interesting source of inspiration for game improvement tips. Here's one on "Driving Tips"—"When choosing a driver, it should look good and feel comfortable in your hands. Swing-weight, length, and flex should all feel right to you. How a club feels is different for each person but the club head should generally always feel light and manageable while still having enough weight to create the feeling of drag. With the right club at hand, there are other considerations to hitting a good tee shot. You should have a slightly closed stance, a low, smooth and wide takeaway and a full turn of the torso. Fifty percent of the ball should be above the club head and it should be positioned ahead in the stance. A full body turn is a must for maximum power. Concentrate on letting the hips and lower back do most of the rotation. A good downswing consists of a smooth pulling action with the hands leading the club through the moment of contact."

Whew, I hope you followed all that. And this is from a golf calendar, written anonymously by the editor, unknown. Instead of Miss September revealed on the page, we get amazing golf tips. We golfers read it for the interesting articles and not the pictures, I believe. Or maybe I'm a bit mixed up after reading popular men's magazines; those are read for the articles, while the golf calendars are perused for the picturesque golf course designs.

Turn to October, here's another brilliant suggestion from the same calendar guru—the heading encourages us to "Focus on a Single Swing Thought"—"When you start to analyze the next shot, your brain gets cluttered and so do your body signals. Don't concern yourself with thinking about past shots or holes. These will only cloud your thinking. Focus solely on the current shot. Select a single swing thought and repeat it to yourself over and over to clear your mind. Then, just as you prepare for your shot, focus all of your attention on breathing in and out, slowly and naturally. This will help you to relax. If other thoughts come to mind, such as 'Did I pick the right driver discussed in September,' let them pass and return to your swing thought. Keep thinking about a single mental cue such as tempo."

This bit of wisdom comes with a very exquisite picture of a course called "Devil's Elbow," shown with a gorge the size of the Grand Canyon bordering the left side of its fairway, and what appears to be one of the Great Lakes down the right side with about twenty yards of green, luscious fairway in between. Be sure to focus all your attention on breathing here and not how many balls you anticipate losing on this unearthly devilish hole, is my advice.

Sigmund Freud or the Dalai Lama himself must have written this calendar tip. *Ommmm, Ommmm*, try to relax, sit in a circle with legs crossed, join hands and sing "Kumbaya" with your foursome on the first tee.

In September, the calendar writers tell us to remember all the idiosyncrasies of hitting the driver, then in October they want a single swing thought. I can't wait to read what November tells us to do. Taking serious tips from a golf calendar is akin to taking driving lessons from a teenager with a learner's permit attempting to drive the family minivan in traffic for the first time. In either case you should be frightened out of your mind, and your chances of ending up in a ditch somewhere are dramatically similar. It is far better to learn golf from an actual golf professional, so I'll take Harry Vardon's advice, which is, "Don't play too much golf; two rounds a day are plenty."

According to several analysts, the golf industry is losing many potential young golfers and the sport overall is in decline. Many youngsters prefer an alternate sport such as soccer where the action is faster and the athlete is more involved with what's happening on the field and gets to chase a speckled black and white ball. Soccer is also a sport where 'soccer mom' or 'soccer dad' patiently waits on the sidelines with fresh cool bottled spring water and chilled slices of fresh oranges for the little tykes. Who wouldn't want that? After running around in circles for ten minutes and getting to kick the ball once, the little darling receives an immediate reward and is then whisked away to the nearest fast food burger joint in order to arrive at the second afternoon event in time—girls' field hockey. At the end of the season, everyone enjoys free pizza and soft drinks, accompanied by a ceremony whereby everyone including the scorekeeper, ball boy or girl receives a gold medallion attached to a ribbon that is displayed around their necks. "And thank you for a great season," the coach says to players and parents.

Many young girls are turning to field hockey, too. Field hockey, irreverently named "running with a stick," is a sport, at least I think it's a sport with which many guys are unfamiliar. It's a team sport, more appropriately called an activity, played primarily by girls clutching short fiberglass sticks with cute designs and appliqués and a curled rounded edge on the bottom. The bottom of the stick resembles the curled-up slippers on the feet of the Wicked Witch in the *Wizard of Oz* when Dorothy's house falls on top of her.

People say that golf is an expensive sport to play. This is not necessarily so or doesn't have to be. Starting out, used golf clubs and golf balls can be found at garage sales anywhere in your community. Practice putting and chipping can be free at local public courses, in your backyard, or an open field. By comparison, field hockey requires an elegant stick, shin guards, a helmet with facemask, elbow and kneepads, and a customized mouth guard, not to mention matching clothing to impress the other participants. Many of these items can be found at secondhand sports stores, with the exception of the mouth guard (yuck, a used chewable plastic spit collector). After spending most of your monthly paycheck on hockey stuff for your offspring, you hope that their interest in this endeavor will last for more than a single season. Contrast this to golf, which is played year-round and enjoyed for a lifetime.

But girls enjoy the camaraderie of a sport such as field hockey. First of all it involves shopping for items needed to play and, more importantly, shopping for fashionable clothing. It also requires huddling in the middle of the field while trying to hit the smallish round ball, which is like a soft cue ball. Inside the huddle formation the girls discuss the unique designs of their sticks and what nice clothing others are wearing. They don't care which team wins, if indeed the score is kept; they have fun, and they are all winners, according to their moms. In golf, the score is kept and every shot recorded, someone wins and usually someone loses, and we don't care what your clubs or clothes look like.

Then there's the activity that's been competing with all sports, which is exercising ones fingers while playing computer and video games. While this is great for hand and finger dexterity, it usually leads to poor interactive communications with others around the gamers. While sitting in the bleachers during one Saturday morning field hockey game, I noticed that more than one-half the attendees were not watching the girls play hockey. These boys and girls, adult men and women, had their heads down and buried into some computer app on their hand held devices. Young people in particular are fast becoming addicted to the little screens at the end of their fingers.

According to an article on *The Wall Street Journal* sports page, which must be important because the WSJ only has one sports page per day, the sport of golf is going on the offensive to attract young players. "One innovation being tested is expanding the hole to fifteen inches to make the sport less psychologically traumatizing. Golf courses are also encouraging golfers to play nine holes, not eighteen." The article continues, "Three might be even better. If golf is to emerge from its state of advanced catalepsy, it must become less rigid, less old-fashioned. In a word, golf needs to be easier."

The editor goes on to say that other sports should follow suit. For example, bowling alleys should make bowling balls larger, get rid of the gutters, bring the pins in a little closer, and make the scoring system simpler for the dummies who can't do fifth grade math. With tongue-in-cheek sarcasm, the editor also suggests that tennis do away with the nets to make play faster and less punishing, or not punishing at all.

Course managers all over the country are scratching their heads trying to find new ways to bring in more players. One local course is having a "Kids Fun Day" with balloons, clowns, a bouncy house play thing, drinks, and a giant twenty-foot inflatable Godzilla reptile that the kids can smack with their club or drive a golf ball into its' belly. This is like the movie *Caddyshack II* on steroids. *Caddyshack II*, a forgettable, tiresome spinoff of the one and only original *Caddyshack*, had millionaire Rodney Dangerfield buying up the beloved Bushwoods Country Club and building condominiums on its fairways. Worst of all, the area of golf course that remained was turned into a golf course-sized miniature course with rotating windmills in the middle of the fairway, clowns jumping out from behind trees and rocks, loud stereo music blasted from giant speakers, and topless female caddies serving drinks to players. I made that last one up, but the movie would have been more memorable if they had been in it. It is hard to remember a single line uttered by any of the actors in this dreadful movie. Other than Dangerfield and maybe Ted Knight, a main character leftover from the original, no other character comes to mind.

Caddyshack the original, on the other hand, set golf apart from other sports in the Eighties and into the Nineties. Every golfer around the world can quote at least one funny line from this iconic movie. If you don't know what "na, na, na, na, na..." means when Chevy Chase said it, or which character says, "It's a Cinderella story," then you are not a dedicated golfer. Please turn in your golf clubs and other paraphernalia and get off the course until you have studied, and can accurately and confidently use, *Caddyshack* movie quotes in the appropriate context.

These fun day gimmicks to lure in the "yoot" of America will not have lasting effects, I'm sure. What they will do, instead, will have unintended consequences such as spoiling the kiddies, who will beg to go to more bounce houses and fun houses where they can get a fruit drink after working up a sweat trying to beat "Golfzilla" to a pulp.

Believe it or not, young people want to be challenged, not coddled into something. As somewhat of an authority on kids' behavior after coaching Little League and high school baseball for more than twenty consecutive years, it is my humble opinion that kids of all ages from around five to eighteen really want to be challenged and have something to reach for. They want to learn new skills and to improve those skills; they don't necessarily want you to make things easier for them. Except math. Kids, in general, hate math at all grade levels. Making the golf hole larger, like fifteen inches wide, is making the game easier, which is opposite of my non-scientific research and hypothesis that kids don't want things easier. It is the adults who want things to be easier for their children when they are struggling, and this thought trickles down to the younger generation. Again, it is my hypothesis.

My wife, Carol, showcasing her PhD in Psychology, chimed in with a similar sentiment. "Making the game easier defeats the purpose of the game. Where's the challenge to a game that is not supposed to be easy? Do baseball players want to hit the ball, a dribbler to the infield, and have it declared a homerun? Do basketball players want to lower the basket to six feet? Instead of all this, course designers should make a 'beginners' golf course, somewhere between a putt-putt miniature and a par 3 course. Here kids and adults of all ages and no skill can go out and have fun while learning the game. Kind of like a 'bunny slope' at a snowy ski resort."

With a smirk, raised eyebrows, and a 'you're so funny' remark, I actually believe this is worthwhile.

One of the nation's top real estate developers and moguls from New York City, Mr. Donald Trump, agrees with me. At least he agrees up to a point. Mr. Trump has bought and built sixteen upscale golf courses and is looking to add more all the time. According to Trump, "We should build up, not build it down. Golf should be an aspirational game, people should aspire to play the game."

"We're bringing the game down with these fifteen inch holes and 'let's play soccer golf.' We should keep it at a high level and not bring it down because a group of people want to sell some more golf clubs or golf balls."

Three cheers for Donald Trump! In essence, he says not to "dumb it down." Let's make golf as it was intended to be all along, with rules established by Old Tom Morris himself. Some rules have been modified to fit the modern game and other rules added for clarification. But a par is still a par, a birdie is still a birdie and, in my case, a bogey is still a bogey. Golfers must be united on this. We don't need a cup on the green the size of a garbage can lid. Aspiring young players should learn and play by the rules.

I can hear ninety percent of you shouting at this page now, "Yeah, right on, brother!! If it was good enough for me then, it's good enough for aspiring golfers now." You are probably also saying, "And I walked five miles to and from school in the ankle-deep snow in winter, uphill, both ways." The other fifty percent of you are shaking your heads, reflecting on your game, staring at the ceiling and saying to no one in particular, "This game is too tough even for adults, let the young'uns have fun."

Where "The Donald" and I differ is on accessibility. He wants courses to be designed and built for the higher achieving professional. He wants exclusivity, or as the investment firm E.F. Hutton once said on national TV, "You errrrrnd it." I think that's all E.F. ever said about making money the old-fashioned way and now Donald Trump is saying it about golf. Clearly though, Donald Trump has been a great ambassador for the game, and you should ask him yourself.

But most of the golfing public wants scenic courses that are affordable for the middle class. Once in a while the average golfer will splurge on one of the "Top 100 Courses You Can Play in the Country" as listed by *Golf Magazine*. On Buddies Trips, vacationing groups tend to play good courses and include one upscale course, maybe even one that's on the list. This is one reason golfers go on these annual trips, in order to play good courses away from home and to occasionally experience a great golf layout. With due respect to Mr. Trump, a popular opinion poll of everyday golfers shows that ninety-two percent want the outing to be affordable and a good time; six percent want to play the best courses no matter the cost, and the rest either didn't care or just wanted to play a round with Michelle Wie or Natalie Gulbis.

I posed this question to a leading Children's Behavior Specialist, a practitioner of child psychology and occasional golfer, frequently found on the course on Wednesday afternoons. This is where I found him during a casual round, so I quizzed him about life in general, about his profession, about children's behavior, and finally zeroed in on my burning desire to know about kids' thinking regarding "life made easier" in America. I was anticipating free advice, from a real shrink.

"Kids today want things handed to them and not to necessarily work hard for them," he began, shredding apart my hypothesis. "However, yours is a misconception that many people have."

"Huh? Are you saying what I'm saying? What is it you are saying anyway, Doc?" I asked.

"Kids of all ages will take what is given to them, and then ask for more of the same because it is faster, simpler, and easier for them. It is natural human behavior to take the shortest road to the desired end result."

"For example, you are now going to ask for a 'gimme' on this next short putt of two to three feet, aren't you?" he predicted, as I came up a little short of my first putt on Hole #7. Damn, it's tough to play with someone who is always reading your thoughts and says stuff out loud before you can.

Yes, I was going to, but can't ask now, you Master of the Mind Game, I thought to myself but didn't say it quite that way.

After tapping in, he asked the question, "What would make you feel more confident and stronger about your golfing skills—me giving you the putt or you yourself working for it and getting it right by hitting the final stroke on the green?"

Man, this guy is good; he turned my question around and is making me answer my own inquiry. "But this isn't about me," I countered as I tried to work my way around the question.

"Oh, but it is about the child in all of us," was his reply.

Dammit, he was in my head again, so I asked him what his handicap was currently, and if he would rather work toward lowering his handicap or would rather play on courses with lower slope ratings. Aha, now the ball was in his court. "What do you say to that one, Doctor Knowitall?"

"I'm just out here to have fun and play the best I know how on the course in front of me, so therein lies the answer to your question about kids, because we are all kids inside."

All of this advice wasn't free after all; he took the five dollar Nassau from me. And my head hurt after all those mind games—I'm not used to thinking so deeply about things I've never thought much about before. At least I didn't have to lie on a couch in his office and spill my guts about what it was like to be a child growing up with six siblings, five older than me. There is not enough time or pages in this chapter or book to address my convoluted upbringing.

Many studies reflect the same idea that the head doctor relayed to me on that golfing Wednesday. However, I have a better, more useful solution to the pressing problem confronting the golfing industry. More accurately, it's a two-part solution to entice more kids to the golf courses.

Solution, Part I:

During our school years, we all remember taking days off from the classroom to travel on a school-sponsored field trip to various places of local interest. Moms packed a sack lunch containing a one-slice baloney sandwich on soggy white Wonder Bread, a very small, fit in the palm of your hand red-green apple that crushed the one item worth it all—the smallish bag of potato chips that Mom had stuffed in a smallish plastic baggie at the bottom of the paper sack. "Today I'm giving you fifty cents for a drink when you get there, so don't lose it."

"Mom, drinks cost more than that."

"So share with Tommy, his mom also gave him fifty cents."

School kids traveled on a frigid yellow bus with cold, clammy, spine-breaking straight-backed seats, with legroom for kids who were four feet tall or shorter. Upon arrival at the "Museum Village of the Damned" or such, one of the studious type girls with a fresh face, freckles, and hair swept up in a tight ponytail would suddenly cry openly and shudder, "I forgot my notebook and pencil to take notes."

"Waaaa, waaaa."

The unfortunate teacher who had the bus duty would try to reassure her that no note taking was necessary. "The kind museum people will have brochures for you to study and carry back home." Not to worry, and please don't cry anymore, and by anymore I mean the rest of the school year. It would later be discovered that the devious, devilish boys in the back of the bus had actually hid Suzie's notebook and pencil just to hear her scream.

At the museum, now for the sixth time in only five years of elementary school, the zombie-like children in Ms. Johnson's fifth grade class would grudgingly walk through the antique buildings built before the Civil War, as illustrated in the shiny trifold handed to the mostly well-behaved children. There was always an unofficial contest proposed by the teachers that judged which of the classes had the most behaved students during the field trip. The winners never, ever got any reward. They were simply declared the winners by an adult chaperone, usually a mom who awarded her own kid's class the title of best behaved class of the day.

On the bus ride back to the school, many of the girls and the egg-headed, geeky boys read the propaganda the museum curator and their assistant curators had handed to each student. They all got two trifolds—one extra to take home to their parents. This also helped the museum to account for the brochures; the more given out the more attendance was recorded. In this way, more county taxpayer money would be budgeted for the museum so that more schools could visit the place in future years.

Others on the bus wadded up their papers and made spitballs to hurl at each other. At the end of the ride, no less than fifteen paper airplanes had been shuffled from the middle of the bus to the back.

Now wasn't that interesting? The same museum, or aquarium in alternate years, has been visited for the ninth time by the students of the twelfth grade.

My solution to the dreaded repetitive field trips taken on worn-out clanky school buses is this—take kids on trips to the local public golf course. Rather than attempting to lure children to golf courses with a carnival on the driving range, course managers can make a deal with school superintendents for these trips. Voila, instant captured audience.

Instead of glossy, colored brochures that the little urchins will use to make spitballs and airplanes, give 'em scorecards. Explain the markings on the scorecard. Now all those classroom days learning math formulas will pay off as they attempt to add up scores. They can be taught the wonderment of how to figure a handicap. More intriguing math formulas! They'll learn new math skills when they slyly subtract strokes from their own scores and add to their playing partners' scores. The math teacher will be thrilled. And so will the English teacher as they learn new vocabulary words. Words like "par," "birdie," "bogey," "over par," "under par," "slice," "hook," "driver," "putter," and "aw shit." They will add new phrases to their diction: "I hate this game," "Golf is a crazy game, ain't it," "Never up, never in," and "Man, where's the cart girl, beer witch?"

Take the children on a tour of the pro shop. There they can "ooooh" and "aaah" over the new golf fashions. Better than a Saturday shopping trip to the mall where they're likely to get in adolescent trouble with the mall cop. They can check out the latest equipment and get great gift ideas for Mother's Day, Father's Day, Grandparents' Day, and my birthday. Let them observe the frustration of the untrained clerk with "Trainee" badge pinned to her shirt behind the counter as she explains the daily green fees with cart included to the uninformed customer. The customer will pay whatever her computer says to pay as she tries to decipher whether it is the morning rate, the afternoon rate, twilight rate, the senior rate, the junior rate, or the couponed rate. With kids observing, this will teach computer skills to the delight of the Technology Advancement teacher.

Now, meet the pro. Unlike the stodgy museum attendant, the pro will take the students on a new and exciting journey. This beats classroom storytelling time, intended to expand the imagination and to kill time during school hours so the frazzled teacher can take a mental break from the chaos. He will engage them with stories of what could have been long ago if he hadn't shanked his approach on Hole #15 on day four of the qualifying tournament. He will tell them about the devastating lower back injury that shortened his promising career on the pro circuit. Kids of all ages will be enthralled to learn of ways to defeat their opponents. The Phys Ed teacher with the closely cropped crew cut and beefy, somewhat flabby upper arms will be beaming, smiling broadly. He's tried to instill a fighting spirit in these kids since Kindergarten.

Next, on to the driving range. Give them a few balls to whack with some old, used clubs. They will love it when their ball bounces off Ramone's leg in the adjoining position. They will learn physics, too. The harder the swing, the worse the result. And the analogous theory, don't mess with Trevor during his backswing or he'll punch you in the arm. School guidance counselors can use this as a study of human behavior. After tormenting on the range, then it is on to the main event.

This is what the students have come for: walking the fairways, learning golf rules and etiquette. The Environmentalists and School Administrators will certainly support this. The very first lesson is, "How to Properly Carry the Golf Bag." Each student gets a lightweight carry bag for this exercise. They learn to sling it over the correct shoulder while maintaining the perfect posture. "No slouching, no slouching!" The Athletic Trainer, no doubt, will shout. She has to, it's her job, and now she can use her "outside voice." Every school these days has one of these professionals, and it's their collective job to correct student posture in the hallways. Here, students are put in a real environment to show off their no-slouch posture and are graded on this exercise. All students receiving "A" or "B" from the trainer will then be placed in the advanced carry bag class. In the next lesson they will carry a slightly heavier bag. These advanced students will be given the ultimate challenge of carrying the professional heavy-duty bag in the very, very advanced bag class. Only a few will achieve this, as studies have shown.

Later they will learn one of the most important etiquette rules. The bag carrying, nature-loving students will be taught how to properly open, then pour, an adult beverage. They must complete this task while holding the bag. They cannot spill any of the beverage in order to move on to the advanced placement. Any spillage will result in a second try on the second hole. After six tries, if a spill occurs, they will receive a grade of "F." This grade will be reported in their academic record and will prevent them from ever landing a future job at McDonalds. Definitely not a job as an airline steward or stewardess, either. It will stain their permanent record.

As the class approaches the greenside bunker on Hole #3, a valuable life's lesson will be given—"How to rake the sand." The parents will benefit from this lesson when their child comes home to perform what they were taught here. Grass clippings are a suitable substitute for sand. Leaves are a perfect alternative. Properly holding the rake is quite important. The skill of developing the correct forearm motion and assuming a tight, not-too-tight, gentle, but firm, grip on the handle will be remembered by the students forever. The proper use of the entire body, focusing on the shoulder, back, and leg muscles, will be explained by the instructor. Each student will perform this activity at the course under the tutelage of the actual Greenskeeper. This is the guy you never see on the course on normal days. What a treat for these kids to meet him and acquire firsthand knowledge from the expert. He will be accompanied by the Assistant Greenskeeper, who will give the lesson. The head Greenskeeper will need to go back to the barn to sharpen his tools and count the remaining number of bags of fertilizer.

The assistant, Artie, wearing an untucked oily grayish white t-shirt with dampened circular sweat stains under the armpits will be chomping on a half-lit stubby cigar as he comes out to greet the youngsters. "I'm Artie, assistant to the head Greenskeeper. If you kids try hard, make it through the tenth grade like I did, and like golf even a little, you can make it big. One of these days soon, I'll have my own assistant and take over as supervisor. Management—that's where it's at."

"Welcome to the third hole, or "my A-hole" as I call it. I take care of it and all the other A-holes. Smitty, the head Greenskeeper who you just met, maintains the B-holes, the other ones. You can learn a thing or two about people by observing the way they take care of their surroundings. Take this here hole for example. It has grass, which is green. And it has sand, which is taupe. Not light brown—taupe. Gotta know the difference. This is what makes you a professional, knowin' the difference. Managers know the difference, and someday I'm gonna be a manager."

You can't learn a lesson like this in the classroom.

After their nine-hole walk among nature, there is excitement in the air. The kids now want to belong. They are salivating to play this game. Or maybe it's because they're hungry. Back at the clubhouse they are treated to all-American fare at the snack bar. These places are given golf-oriented names like "Bogeys," "the 19th Hole," and "At the Turn." Here golfers can munch on six-dollar hot dogs, nine dollar hamburgers, or fifteen dollar ham and swiss sandwiches. You can't go wrong with the club sandwich; every one I've ever had at these places has been an epicurean delight. For the price of a small European car, you can order a decent lunch meal. It comes with fries, of course.

"Hey kids, no sack lunches here. And you don't have to share your soda. Just bring a wheelbarrow full of cash and enjoy."

Once schools start taking my approach, more young players will be headed to the great outdoors of the nearby driving range.

Solution, Part II:

The second part of my solution (remember, there are two parts to this) is quite simple and genius at the same time. Offer "happy hour" prices to adults and their tagalong kids. The kids don't even have to be their own kids, just kids from the neighborhood or kids from school. Adults pay half price, and kids can play for free. That's right—free!

To be honest this isn't a new concept, it was originated long before my revelation. In the ice cream business for five decades, my dad started this many years ago. To any parent wanting a little smidgen of ice cream for their baby to try, Dad would offer them a "baby cone" of ice cream at no charge. As all babies love ice cream, they would lap it up in front of their adoring parents. Parents overly appreciated the free stuff, though who doesn't, and vowed to return. Many, if not all, did. This was a genuine marketing scheme that has continued for all these years. The babies became voracious teenagers able to eat an entire vat of ice cream. As the teenagers would gather in mobs, we'd have packs of them slurping milkshakes and demolishing banana splits. As these customers morph into adults, they return with their children for the freebies. The cycle of ice cream consumption continues, all because of a bite-sized dollop of it handed out years ago.

The golf industry can learn from this.

Many local bars and restaurant owners exclaim that "happy hour" brings in new and repeat customers. Heck, yeah, folks like bargains. Golf course managers, those who are desperate for young blood to play their venue, can offer lower prices during after-school hours for adults and the draw of "free" for school children. Opinion polls are definite on this fact—Golf has gotten too expensive to play.

There is one golf course in Virginia, King Carter Club in Irvington, which has caught on to this idea. They advertise, "Free golf with the purchase of a hot dog." This is excruciatingly clever on their part, something that catches attention immediately. The cost of the hot dog is just thirty-five dollars.

There ya' go. A two-part solution to the low attendance on golf courses, and the general decline of golf that is ailing the industry. Older golfers are sincerely happy with the way things are now, however. These are the "get off my lawn" curmudgeons telling you that nobody wants a crowded tee box and six-hour rounds. "Shhhhh, you'll ruin the game, daag-nabit."

One interesting factoid revealed by friends and others involves found golf balls. An unwritten rule that is passed down from generations of golfers and found mostly to be true is this: When you find someone else's lost ball in the woods or high rough, you should not use that found ball during the current round. Certainly do not use that ball within the next three holes of play. Simple laws of physics dictate that if it is used on the same day it is found, it will be lost by you, the new owner. It is hard to resist using the found ball, since it is immediately placed in your pants pocket and is at the ready. But resist you must. You are already in the woods or rough because that is where you located the ball. The law of physics applied here is "An object in motion tends to stay in motion, while an object at rest tends to stay at rest." The ball found in the rough has come to rest, perhaps for days, and it should remain so.

An example of this law is observed in several unlikely places. Many office managers and business executives own the familiar desk accessory apparatus consisting of five small steely balls dangling from two v-shaped strings for visitors to admire. When the outermost shiny silver ball is released to hit the others, the three balls nearest the center stay in place, only to have the farthest silver ball escape away after the clacking sound. As it returns with its own clack, the ball on the opposing side then slips away in a never-ending litany of clack, clack, clack, clack, and continues until the observer has had enough and finally ends the clacking misery.

The corollary theory of finding a lost ball is a situation in which you are the loser of the ball. It goes like this: When you lose a ball, never drop a brand new ball in its place. Do not take out a fresh sleeve of balls and use one to replace the lost one. It too will be lost almost immediately, and no one wants to lose a four dollar Titleist just purchased in the pro shop before the round. The same law of physics is applied in this case, because the new golf ball has nestled in among new friends in the golf bag pouch and is comfortably at rest. It has to wait its rightful turn, as the older balls are eager to be released into the outside world.

As you trample through the woods looking for lost balls, be wary and careful at the same time of the wildlife and insects found there. Consider that woods, weeds, and underbrush is the home course for these inhabitants. Those annoying little ticks and chiggers cling to your skin and everything you are wearing. Somehow they manage to jump up midway up your legs, cling to your calf or farther up to the waist under the belt line area without notice. Biologists inform us that these bugs seek darkened and moist places on the human body; therefore, we should wear light colored clothing. It is a nice thought, but doesn't actually work that way. I'll never forget the time when I came out of the deep woods after searching for a wayward drive and instantly feeling itching sensation over both ankles. By the time I got home my ankles where the top of my full- length white cotton socks stopped, both legs were totally reddened and blistered from the onslaught of chiggers. And I'd only been in the brush for not more than five minutes, max. Ooooh, the itching and burning from those little microscopic buggers. *Don't scratch, don't scratch*, I kept telling myself, scratching them makes it worse, and I convinced myself that they spread when scratched. After a soothing shower, I wrapped both legs up to the lower calves in an old tee shirt soaked in rubbing alcohol. Those chiggers came screaming out, or at least they were probably screaming, hopefully they were screaming, to run away from my alcohol-induced skin. My ankles looked like raw mashed up hamburger meat, the kind that is mixed before going into the oven to make meatloaf. And mine had secret sauce added, creamy liquefied puss mingled with the scent of alcohol on the white, now discolored, t-shirt around the infected areas. It took five days to recover from the itch-fest. Since that episode, I have carried a spray can of industrial strength "Deet" insecticide in my bag, and when entering the wood line, I spray around me desperately trying to kill off as many friends of the chiggers that infected me earlier. If their associates, the ticks, become collateral damage, well too bad for them for being an accessory to the crime.

The larger animals are easier to recognize and to avoid for the most part. Those noisy honking Canadian Geese are the most malodorous beasts found everywhere nowadays except in Canada. They need to go back to their homeland. Geese, you are welcome to visit during the winter months in the lower forty-eight states when there are fewer golfers outside, but like the relative who comes for a three day stay, ends up in your house for two weeks, you are no longer welcome. Go home, as Mother Nature intended. With no offense intended to our northern neighbors, these geese are nasty birds that leave large smelly, sticky droppings on beautifully manicured fairways and greens. Unlike other wild animals, these birds come in flocks, never individually where you can arbitrarily shoo them away. They are a protected species, no longer on the endangered list as they once were twenty years ago. It really should be the other way around; it should be the golfer who is protected from these invaders. They stand their ground, bellow at you if you came near, and charge your cart like a medieval jousting match. The golfer has paid the daily fees, and the geese get to graze on whatever they eat in the grasses. We all would like you to take a lesson from your distant cousins, the ducks. Mallards hang around in ponds and creeks, then fly north bound in summer.

I'm a nature lover and don't want to harm these birds, just want them back in their natural habitat. My backyard overlooks a wide marsh, protected wetlands, and a tidal creek where plenty of nature's beauties live and come to visit during the seasons. I watch them with binoculars from my porch, from a distance, and can identify several species found in my Audubon Society birding book. I feed them all year long with three fully stocked bird feeders. They are all very beautiful and welcome, but the Canadian Geese don't know their boundaries. If animals have criminals among them, these geese would commit the most felonies; so to these honkers, we all say, "Get the flock outta here."

If it is agreeable with you, may I take one more mulligan? I'm begging here, but you don't really have a choice in this decision.

All the tales you have read were real, with some slight alterations or embellishments. You just can't make this stuff up, as life happens. The tournaments, the games, the events, the discussions, the situations, the course locations, the oddball personalities are how I remembered them.

About half of the characters names are their actual names, others are not quite as written, but their actions were theirs alone. Carol, my wife, is Carol; Sarah, my daughter and Zoey, the granddaughter, are Sarah and Zoey; the three Patrick's are who they are; Tom "Muunroe" Rogers, T. Foster, "Moose," "Jaybird," Scotty Dez, Mikey, Oldham Daryl, Mr. D, Boat, Roger, Private Buford and the guys in Chapter 9, Gadgets, are themselves. As one NFL head coach of the Arizona Cardinals once asserted in a media conference after a playoff game, "They are who we thought they were." Others in the book have new imagined names, which were inserted to protect their identity.

For all these folks, thank you for many memorable times over the past forty years that are retold in these pages. Hopefully, there will be forty more years of golfing memories that will be published as *More Characters on the Green*.

Index

"Fixing your slice...", Moe Norman Golf, www.squareto-squaremethod.com, Oct 2014

Levelhead Marker, www.iron-lagolf.com, Nov 2014

Nike Lunar Control 3, www.golfweek.com, Jan 2015, and www.golf.com , Jan 2015

Chapter 10: Hank-Enstein and the Dark side

P 147, Ultimate Jox Sox, internet ad

p. 149, Lesson BogeyPro Series, www.BogeyPro.com

"What does the Way You Walk Say About You?" Cindi May, *Scientific American*, Oct 2012

"Snap, Making the Most of First Impressions", Patti Wood, *Huffington Post Canada*, by Jacqueline Delange, May 2012

Chapter14: Mulligans

"Focus on Single Swing Thought", *Golf Tips 2014*, *Calendar*, COMDA Advertising Connections, www.comda.com

"DrivingTips", GolfTips, *2014, Calendar*, COMDA Advertising Connections, www.comda.com

Expanding the hole to 15 inches. "Moving Targets: Joe Queenan", *Wall Street Journal*, April 26, 2014

Donald Trump interviews, *Golf Channel*, April 2014, and Golf.com, May 14, 2014

Acknowledgements

In order to make these episodes explode onto the pages, I had to start with many real golfers. Playing for the past forty years, I have included golfing buddies and friends who have inspired some interesting golf memories.

"Air Force Patrick" Downey, "Army Patrick" Taylor, Patrick "Dizmo" Disney, Tom "T" Foster, Tom "Monroe" Rogers, Jim "Scottso" Scott, S.W. "Moose" Spencer, Mike "Mikey" Seger, Bob "Dizzy Bob" Williams, Scott "Dez" Desrosiers, my sister Anne Hoyer, and friend Linda "the Liberal" Webster. Posthumously, Cousin Charlie "Cha-Lee" Kodidek, and my old Army Platoon Sergeant, mentor and friend, SFC Roger M. Withrow.

The professionals who helped review and encouraged my writing, so you can blame them if you have to. Nick Zanca at Kiskiack Golf Club, Andy Weissinger, PGA at the Pines, Ft. Eustis, Trish Williams, Bob Voss, first editor Megan Silvas who made these words into understandable sentences, and senior editor Carol Thompson, a genuine pro.

Above all are the folks closest to me and endured many hours of my "thinking out loud" sessions and requests for constructive criticisms. Believe me, they gave their best shots. My wife Carol, daughter Sarah, son Chris, and granddaughter Zoey. Thank you all and I love you.

Almost forgot, Private Buford the bulldog, who is now in the care of my son Chris and his wife Angie.

CPSIA information can be obtained
at www.ICGtesting.com
Printed in the USA
BVHW070014160322
631486BV00002B/76